Writing and the Body in Motion

ALSO BY CHERYL PALLANT

Contact Improvisation: An Introduction to a Vitalizing Dance Form (McFarland, 2006)

Writing and the Body in Motion
Awakening Voice through Somatic Practice

CHERYL PALLANT

McFarland & Company, Inc., Publishers
Jefferson, North Carolina

All photographs are by Tania Fernandez / Strawberry St Photography

LIBRARY OF CONGRESS CATALOGUING-IN-PUBLICATION DATA

Names: Pallant, Cheryl, author.
Title: Writing and the body in motion : awakening voice through somatic practice / Cheryl Pallant.
Description: Jefferson, North Carolina : McFarland & Company, Inc., Publishers, [2018] | Includes bibliographical references and index.
Identifiers: LCCN 2018004068 | ISBN 9781476668246 (softcover : acid free paper) ∞
Subjects: LCSH: Dance—Psychological aspects. | Body image. | Mindfulness (Psychology)
Classification: LCC GV1588.5 .P35 2018 | DDC 792.8019—dc23
LC record available at https://lccn.loc.gov/2018004068

BRITISH LIBRARY CATALOGUING DATA ARE AVAILABLE

ISBN 978-1-4766-6824-6 (print)
ISBN 978-1-4766-3171-4 (ebook)

© 2018 Cheryl Pallant. All rights reserved

No part of this book may be reproduced or transmitted in any form or by any means, electronic or mechanical, including photocopying or recording, or by any information storage and retrieval system, without permission in writing from the publisher.

Front cover image of Relational connecting: reaching outward and inward simultaneously (Tania Fernandez / Strawberry St Photography)

Printed in the United States of America

McFarland & Company, Inc., Publishers
  Box 611, Jefferson, North Carolina 28640
  www.mcfarlandpub.com

Acknowledgments

Over the years, this book has gone through various versions that draw from my Writing from the Body classes and reflect the development of my own movement, writing, and meditation practice and those of my students, workshop participants, and clients. I want to thank them for undertaking a somatic journey and sharing their experiences with me. Thanks to Terry Dolson, in particular, for your heartfelt story.

I want to thank those who agreed to be photographed for this book: Celina Alvarez, Aaron Brown, Amy Impellizzeri, Robbie Kinter, Feivel Nihm, John Swift, and Yao Thompson. You followed instructions gracefully. Thanks to the amazing Tania Fernandez for your professionalism in easily zooming in on moving bodies which are more challenging than stationary subjects. Your quick eye knows well where to look and how to match words with images.

Thanks to Beth Parsons who recognized what my lines were trying to convey and could readily identify an error. Thanks to Don for your ongoing encouragement, the piles of books, your dedication to evolving, and, despite the chaos of writing a book, for going ahead with marrying me.

The body is living art. Your movement through time and space is art. A painter has brushes. You have your body.
—Anna Halprin

Words bounce. Words, if you let them, will do what they want to do and what they have to do.
—Anne Carson

Dance first. Think later. It's the natural order.
—Samuel Beckett

Table of Contents

Acknowledgments v
Preface 1
Introduction 5

1. The Subjective Body 15
2. The Perceiving Body 38
3. The Kinesthetic Body 61
4. The Verbal Body 88
5. The Imagining Body 113
6. The Evolutionary Body 137
7. The Practicing Body 159

Glossary 171
Chapter Notes 173
Bibliography 176
Index 179

Preface

I must dance. I must write. On first glance, these disciplines appear unrelated and incompatible. On the surface it would seem that dance relies solely on the body and writing relies exclusively on the mind and never the twain shall meet. Each discipline requires ample time and effort devoted to build skill. Over the years, well intentioned teachers and colleagues advised me to choose one or the other. I tried. Yet as soon as I chose one, the other returned like a scorned lover knocking on the door with hopes of winning back my affections. Once the door opened, I recognized the error in my decision and the relationship resumed.

My love of writing began early. By fourth grade a closet shelved my notebooks filled with my musings, stories, and poems. Any time a teacher assigned a story to write for homework, the next day my classmates urged me to read my completed work aloud. They knew my writing contained vivid detail that rendered my stories believable. Mostly I shared my writing with a select audience, my best friend who lived next door and my cat who listened by sitting upright and then belly flat upon the paper once I set it down.

I had a fertile imagination, fed by reading books and adventuring into thousands of acres of woods behind my house. Pages turned and steps taken onto leaves and broken branches colored my imagination with larvae, moles, arrow heads, Seussian rhymes, and a shy stegosaurus. I could sit for hours watching a spider weave its web and catch an unsuspecting beetle. Day after day I monitored the trickle or rush of a stream by whether I crossed with an easy hop or a catapulted leap and sometimes splash. I spent entire mornings curled under my blanket in bed, unwilling to put my book down or close my journal, doing so only at the beckoning of my mom insisting I attend to household chores.

Hikes into the woods, reading, and writing took me places beyond the familiarity of my house and family. I regularly traveled by both word and foot, my hunger for encounters opening me to witness and participate in the wonders of life. Writing came naturally and continued over the years, my notebooks a guaranteed stage and consummate audience who encouraged exploration, expression, and my quest to understand the world.

Dance entered my life in college. The course catalog listed a class in creative movement which I signed up for on a whim. I did so in defiance of a doctor who at the start of high school labeled me disabled because of a diagnosis of scoliosis, a curved spine, and discouraged my participation in dance and gym. To avoid the need to wear a brace or be encased by a cast during high school, I had maintained a rigid posture to prevent the worsening of my curvature. Pain, my doctor warned, would be with me for life.

Movement would change everything.

Initially, I entered dance class lethargically, my body stiff, my energy droopy. It took great effort to battle inertia and learned passivity and be able to carry out small exercises like lifting my right leg for ten counts, then my right leg, then twisting or bending. "More," insisted my teacher, "bigger." On some days the thought of packing a bag with dance clothes for the exertion to follow felt overly burdensome. I persisted, though. I persisted because each class noticeably shifted me. I would walk across campus with a new levity and heightened alertness for my studies. I developed a curiosity about my body and its abilities. My invisible brace had unlocked and was slipping off. I felt renewed, as if flinging windows and doors open after a long, oppressive storm.

As my strength and range of motion increased in the dance studio, my experiences in the world shifted. I came to recognize the link between how I moved in the world and how the world moved me. I was learning what it felt like to move with freedom and joy, to feel open and engage actively with each moment. Colors intensified, shapes sharpened, and thoughts ignited. Attending to my body and feeling its many sensations rooted me in the present moment. My newly found creative outlet captured my attention and pointed toward an interdependency between the mind and the body. Significantly, the shackle to lifelong back pain predicted by my doctor proved impermanent, the pain lessening with every dance class. Years later the pain disappeared entirely.

As an English major, I spoke little about my dual involvement with professors who, depending on their field of dance or English, either put down the body or put down books. The Cartesian battle raged with me on the front lines waving the white flag. There was no way I was going to give up either involvement.

Graduate school showed me the first of many ways movement and writing complement each other. I was sitting at the desk in my apartment writing my thesis. Fifty pages into the paper, the writing stopped. I stared at the blank page hoping concentration alone would generate the next paragraph, but no combination of ink and willpower worked. When no words appeared the rest of afternoon nor the next day, panic set in. Deadlines loomed. There was no time for idling.

On impulse, I got up from my chair. I looked around the room at the design of the window grid and the dried flowers in a vase. As was the custom in dance class, my focus turned to feeling the press of my feet upon the floor. My breath changed, deepened, and a small dance blossomed near the table, then the dresser and the bed as I settled by chance upon a pace and rhythm that contrasted the writing stranglehold. A necessary shift occurred and inspiration for writing returned. I headed back to my chair.

This pattern of alternating writing with movement, attention to thought and words with attention to body and movement, carried me through to the final page and successful completion of my thesis. But something else took hold during that period, curiosity about how these disciplines may be complementary.

Curiosity led to numerous interdisciplinary performances and writing several cross-genre books. Curiosity led to learning about many forms of improvisational dance such as Contact Improvisation, Authentic Movement, and 5 Rhythms; to somatic practices such as Body-Mind Centering, Continuum, Tai Chi, Trager Mentastics and Alexander Technique; to energy healing modalities such as Reiki and Healing Touch. Curiosity led to understanding that movement is helped by writing and writing is helped by movement. Curiosity led to further explore an already formed meditation practice, to embodied states of consciousness, and to the recognition of a life-affirming energy that is personal and universal, fleeting and transformative, and core to the well being. The body contained mystery, but it also supplied gifts.

Findings from these investigations made their way into creating Writing from the Body, the class I teach semester-long and as a workshop around the country and abroad. This book draws heavily from that material. It looks at the ways dancing and writing work together with somatic awareness to create a synergy that yields powerful results. This potent combination leads to new material in movement and in writing, to insights, wisdom, consciousness, and healing. It supports finding out who we are and who we can become. It supports living in our body with embodied awareness and knowing. It supports thriving in our personal, subjectively felt body with an awareness of the mutual influence of the collective body.

This book is an invitation to deep bodily listening. It invites you to open your senses, to listen deeply to your body and your words, to come to know your somatic, relational self, and to suspend usual preconceptions and expectations. It invites you to journey to follow the motion, meaning, and sinews of your own curiosity.

Introduction

We all move. We all write.

We are always in motion. Each day, we turn in bed, prepare food in the kitchen, walk the hallway to work, twist knobs, push doors, grab, bend, hoist, and essentially perform an endless series of movements. We also frequently write—notes, texts, emails—and read what's written—billboards, books, t-shirt slogans. Movement and words surround us. They appear throughout the day so commonplace that they may barely register, their full impact escaping notice.

Behind every movement and every word is a motivation. A person brings the movement and word to the foreground with the aim to communicate. Sometimes that communication is deliberate and intentional. Other times it slips out with little awareness.

Those who actively embrace dancing and writing are commonly referred to as dancers and writers. In pursuing these mediums with diligence, they achieve agility and grace. They seemingly easily create works of beauty or provocation. To identify as a dancer or writer, however, especially at the start, typically rouses a charged response. "Me? Oh, not me. I'm such a klutz," we say. And "I fumble with words all the time." Admiring the grace of dancers and writers, we secretly hope for similar heights for ourselves. We hope an unknown force will miraculously propel us to the same abilities as those we admire and our skills will develop.

My intention in this book is to inspire and provide you with ways to further your skills in moving and writing, to reach greater expressive ability from this combination. My intention, also, is to lead you to increasing your somatic awareness, to come to know yourself, and the power that comes with that embodied knowing.

Labels can create unnecessary obstacles. They're problematic when they elicit an ideal for which our self-worth, if underestimated, falls short. They're problematic if we habituate toward self-criticism without offsetting it with a healthy dose of encouragement. Labels can entangle us with ego and restrict free expression and experimentation. With this in mind, note that I will periodically write "movement practitioner," "dance practitioner," or "writing practitioner," all of which emphasizes the practice, not identity nor results from the disciplines.

My dance background arises out of recognizing complex movement patterns as well as simple pedestrian movements as dance. Rising up from a chair can be a dance. Lifting then lowering an arm can be a dance. Similarly, a poem may be five words or five stanzas long, impromptu or planned. The writing may drip with personal truths without adhering to any standard of craft or compel with elegant forms. For these reasons, I encourage deep listening and the embrace of raw creative energy.

Deep listening occurs at a fundamental level and puts the focus on actions moment to moment, not the judgements about those actions. Deep listening relies on curiosity and discerning the differences between judgement and sensory input. Deep listening emphasizes noticing and perceiving sensations, not judging them as good or bad, but addressing them with open awareness.

As practitioners of a craft, we are perpetual students which I believe is the best perspective for staying connected to the life pulse and to creativity. Practitioners are continually opening themselves to new experiences and new approaches. Buddhists use the concept of Beginner's Mind to signify ongoing learning, possibilities of presence, and avoiding being stuck in judgement and binary, dualistic right/wrong thinking. As practitioners, we raise questions, immerse ourselves, and pursue a path. Over time, the lessons of our practice create a body of work that is both helpful and harmful. The helpfulness takes place when we accomplish a task, create results with ease, and learn along the way. Harm occurs when we fall into habits which dull the senses, minimize creativity, and weaken the life pulse. Astute practitioners know to hang on to past lessons but also to welcome coming to know changing present circumstances.

Awareness is key. Awareness happens when focus turns to body and sensation, when we quiet a loud mind or give voice to a hushed one, when we notice the movement in stillness and the stillness in motion. Awareness happens when we alter our speed, rearrange a usual sequence, or shift context. Awareness happens when we feel into areas previously hidden, when we notice our breath and our biases, when we allow comfort and discomfort and learn what it means to be present.

The Chinese character for listening refers not only to the ears, but also the eyes, heart and mind. This type of listening, somatic and syncretic, is a full body experience. In deep listening, we find out to what degree we engage with living. Options show up. Relief and possibility show up. Creative expression, there all along, appears.

Combining Dancing with Writing

Dance practitioners know well the benefits that come from movement: strength, flexibility, coordination, balance, confidence. Dancing develops kinesthetic, proprioceptive, and spatial know-how. The visceral immediacy of dancing leads to a personal bodily intelligence.

Writing practitioners develop specialized skills as well, an analytic and verbal pliancy and the ability to assign words to fit experience. Writing establishes a verbal vocabulary for developing imagination and proves useful in communicating complex ideas. Each practice alone is powerful in its contribution to developing joy and a creative muscle. Each deepens engagement with day to day existence and contributes to self-knowing, self-awareness, and expressive ease.

The particulars of each discipline builds upon the other. Together they provide numerous benefits regardless of skill. The combination of dancing with writing, however, is especially potent and creates a rare synergy. The combination helps in

- Articulating experience and furthering that articulation.
- Generating new dance and writing experiences and material.
- Uniting parts of the brain to increase alertness and overall effectiveness.
- Increasing problem solving, discovering new solutions, and supporting integrative thinking.
- Establishing flow, coherence, and well-being.
- Embracing creative, generative energy and establishing new meaning.
- Supporting embodied knowing and expression, expansive being, and intersubjectivity.
- Raising human potential for increased consciousness, innovation, evolution, and sustainability.

Whether they initially engage the material with an open mind or with cynicism, participants in my classes and workshops regularly astound themselves. They create new material and insights that surpasses expectation. The unimagined manifests. Possibilities sticking to the sidelines take center stage. The Aha! of discovery and wonder occurs.

The combination of moving and writing brings the energy of mind into coherence with the energy of the body. The power of this synergy surpasses the output of material created from a single discipline. The synergy dredges up material from the personal and collective unconscious and shows it in a light that is resonant, fresh, and empowering. As a synergetic discipline based on subjective experience, this material is individual as well as integrative.

Articulation

Each discipline separately articulates experience. Movement engages the space of the body with surrounding space and generates particular motions required to perform an action. Writing works similarly in that words are tried until the best phrasing is chosen. The process of definition contributes to heightening senses. The heightened senses extend our ability to express. In understanding parts—any of the parts—the whole comes into greater clarity.

With clarity comes options. Once we know what goes into a phrase in either movement or words, we can make alterations. The stretch deepens when we lower the shoulder muscle, for instance. Similarly, we can provide more detail about the canoe drifting down river and the words chosen to describe it when we feel "drift" in our body.

Options liberate us from always doing something the same way. We discern the difference between reacting versus responding to conditions. We come to understand what works and why. When we get into flow, the components are more richly informed than if we hadn't investigated them.

Combining the disciplines can be daunting initially. Some choose dance to avoid the need to use words. Conversely some choose to write to avoid the awkwardness of movement and sensing the body. One discipline may prove easier than the other for many. Yet how do you accurately describe a movement? How do you move if you see yourself as uncoordinated?

Weakness in one discipline is strengthened by experience with the other. Blending them contributes to increased overall confidence and ability.

The combination brings forth layers of experience of what it means to be a body. The combination deepens understanding and embodiment. The body, otherwise nonverbal, selects words and is voiced. The voice moves, feels sensation, emotions, and links intimately with body. Writing fleshes out. Writing resonates. Movement treads new territory. Awareness expands. Understanding movements deepens. Understanding writing deepens. Being embodies.

Thinking takes place with the body *and* the mind. Phrasing in word or motion builds from a robust, felt foundation. Words fill with flesh and flesh filled words establish a firm, embodied foundation. Increased literacy takes place in motion and word along with a greater dexterity with both.

Generating the New

We may have taken up one of these disciplines as an outlet for the joy that accompanies creative expression or the need for relief from daily stresses. A creative path helps define who we are and supports growth. Creative expression provides the impetus and means to navigate the rugged terrain and challenges of living. These reasons alone provide substantive motivation to pursue a creative path.

It's good to be reminded that creative expression is seldom a linear path. We do not go to the studio once and leave an hour later with a fully formed dance. Rarely do we sit down at the computer and generate a coherent piece of crafted writing from a single attempt.

Creative expression is a messy business. It requires multiple trials and attempts that are less than glorious. The route is circuitous, winding, bumpy, usually longer than is preferred. Accept its chaos and uncertainty and the process itself becomes rewarding. Each step along the way offers rich detail, moments unfolding a creative feast, truths tied to embodiment, and opportunities to deepen breath and understanding as well as imaginative visions and innovative solutions.

Some of the ideas and exercises that you'll encounter in this book may provoke discomfort. Bring it on, I say! Discomfort could be a sign of upending an outmoded understanding and way of accomplishing an action. Discomfort signals us to pay attention. Heightened attention leads to new findings, creativity, and growth. Disorientation is a precursor to reorientation. Learning takes place after a period of confusion, after a set of behaviors gets replaced. Persist through the discomfort and rewards big and small show up.

The ideas and practices in this book are process, not product oriented. Process focuses on the events and insights that take place along the way. The focus is the journey, not the destination. That said, you will also find new techniques to hone your craft.

Languages and the Brain

Movement and writing are both languages, a way to engage with and order existence. A language is a common set of symbols and signs that assist in making sense of the world. A language is essential for communication. It provides an avenue for leaving our isolated existence and connecting with the larger world.

Howard Gardner's theory of multiple intelligences delineates the value of identifying our innate language, what he defines as a primary sensory mode or intelligence. Typically, we demonstrate greater ability in one sensory mode over others. Those who dance regularly develop high kinesthetic intelligence. Those who write regularly develop high linguistic intelligence. Identifying fluency in a particular sensory mode and matching it to a situation helps in improving learning and engagement. But here's where the ideas within these pages prove especially useful: combine a strong intelligence with a weaker one and not only does the latter benefit, but so does the former. It becomes an interdisciplinary practice, a type of bilingualism that contributes to an expansion of learning and understanding.

Brain scans show that many regions of the brain, primarily the motor cortex and cerebellum, are activated while dancing. The parietal lobe is largely responsible for writing. Combine moving and writing and the lights of the brain imaging machines show more areas illuminated.[1] Moving and writing increases neuronal activity and brain plasticity and prepares us for facing challenges with greater ability and adaptability. This book will turn on your lights and help increase the frequency of your illuminations.

Moving with Somatic Awareness

Every nuance of the body is an event unto itself and a pivotal bridge to new material, new understanding, and embodiment. Every nuance is the prima matera of identity and its expression. With awareness comes learning how we move, what frees us and what holds us back. The path to options and creative expression opens up.

Moving with somatic awareness is an inside out looking. The emphasis is on proprioception and an intimate knowing of the emotions and mechanics of our body. The inside out perspective runs into the history contained by our personal body. What occurs below consciousness is brought to the foreground. The difference between habitual movement for which little attention is paid and open, consciously chosen movement is made clear. The latter way of moving opens us to choice. Moving with awareness ushers in insights, creative possibility and new movement.

The relationship with self shifts. In deep listening to our personal body moving, we come home to our own body as both witness and doer. The body provides a constant stream of sensations for us to perceive. In feeling our sensations, we find out what is and what is not us, which patterns from the past are no longer useful, and how to adapt to the present, all of which leads to moving with greater efficiency.

Writing from the Body Versus Writing About the Body

Commonly we write *about* the body. The body is viewed as a thing, an object. It has basic needs like eating and sleeping, but we give it minimal sensory attention for the most part, unless we get sick and then we pay it inordinate attention to alleviate the symptoms. The attention, however, is neither global nor nuanced.

In writing *about* the body, the body as object could be any body. We may write about fingers, abdominal pain, or gender but the approach is through objectification. Regardless of the body topic, the writing takes place with an emphasis on thought. With attention on thinking, we may overlook the body, our personal body, that is. Our felt idiosyncratic sensations are left behind.

There is great value in writing *about* the body, especially to explore parts of us that receive little attention. It helps to investigate our body through a cultural and biological lens for instance. The hard and soft sciences contain decades' worth of valuable information to assist in understanding this mass of flesh that is us.

This book also includes ideas and exercises for writing *from* the body, positioning the body as subject. This prepositional shift, the "about" to "from" is significant. Prepositions establish relationships, typically between a noun (or pronoun), in this case us, and an object. The "about" places the body outside us whereas the "from" positions the body inside. We write *with* the body. We rely on felt experiences and the personal energy of the body in the moment of its occurrence. We write from the intimacy of first-hand experience before there's an opportunity to conceptualize.

The writing *from* is subjective and personal. We follow impulses of the body. We are the impulses of the body. Writing is the movement. The method reinforces straying from known conventions and forms of expression into forms and truths that may be less familiar. It may appear as fragments or as a swirl of words across the page.

How to Use This Book

Chapter 1, "The Subjective Body," looks at the field of somatics as established by Thomas Hanna and how the technique of combining movement with writing builds upon his foundational ideas. Moving and writing by themselves are each considered transformative activities, but their combination is offered as a way to deepen somatic awareness.

Chapter 2, "The Perceiving Body," is a discussion of perceptions that goes beyond the usual five senses of sight, sound, touch, smell, and taste. Presented are alternative models of perception. Included are awareness channels and intelligences that illustrate how the world is perceived and what is possibly perceivable.

Chapter 3, "The Kinesthetic Body," focuses on movement and sensation and the importance of developing a practice of being able to read the signs provided by the body. A literacy with reading such cues leads to choices that can enhance our lives. Discussed are the benefits of noticing what takes place with a body in stillness and in motion.

Chapter 4, "The Verbal Body," looks at writing and shows how languaging the body articulates somatic awareness. The writing is framed as a perceptual pathway as well as a way to further embodied knowing. Writing combined with a subjective awareness of how we use words tied to flesh is considered critical to embodiment.

Chapter 5, "The Imagining Body," looks at the importance of imagination and the usefulness of symbols and metaphors. These are used to access the unconscious, to transform the raw hidden material and bring it to consciousness. Imagination is seen as a path to developing embodied knowing.

Chapter 6, "The Evolutionary Body," shifts from an individual to a collective focus and how this perspective correlates to the sustainability of people and the Earth. Awareness is viewed through a developmental, social, spiritual, and evolutionary lens and touches on issues such as sexism and panpsychicism.

Chapter 7, "The Practicing Body," is devoted exclusively to exercises to further your somatic inquiry and journey.

At the close of every chapter are exercises for moving and writing with somatic awareness. The exercises are referred to within the body of the chapter as well, so you can match ideas with practice. The majority of the exercises can be done alone, with several that require a second person or a small group. A glossary can be found at the back of the book.

You have options for proceeding through the book. You can read each chapter sequentially as it is laid out and perform the exercises as they appear or upon completion of the chapter when the ideas are still fresh. I recommend this approach to familiarize yourself with the ideas and then to personalize them. This approach allows you to shift frequently between objective and subjective perspectives, my views alongside your experiences and reflections. A second, wholly different approach is to focus exclusively on the exercises in each chapter and upon completion, return to the beginning of the book and compare your experiences with the ideas presented in each chapter.

If any exercise is particularly stirring, challenging or fruitful, I urge you to repeat it. All exercises are meant as guidelines. Modify them to your circumstances and learn to follow the wisdom of your body.

To maximize comfort, select a room where you can close the door to distractions. Lock the door if necessary. The room need not be clear of furniture but should have an area of floor that is unobstructed and spacious enough for movement. Sit. Take a few deep breaths. Every session begins this way. Find a position that is comfortable. To prepare your body to explore, set an intention, which is discussed in Chapter 1, and do a simple warm up, discussed in Chapter 3. Use music for the movement exercises if you want. Your choice of music, its rhythms and melody, for instance, influences your movement so choose carefully. Consider trying them with and without music.

At times my language is specific. For example: Lift an arm to shoulder height and hold for five minutes. Other times, my language is abstract and poetic and requires interpretation. My intention is to guide you, but also let you find your own way. Be aware of my suggestions, but more importantly, use them to develop and ultimately lead to your own guidance.

The chapters include anecdotes from my students, workshop participants, and energy healing clients. The names given are not their real names. Several wished to remain anonymous and for the sake of aesthetic consistency, I refer to them all with a pseudonym.

I write this book with the hope that it inspires your body to awake to its vitalizing currents as you become your best self. Consider this an invitation. I hope that you can stand tall in your body and twist and bend and lounge as needed. I hope that you learn the differences between sensing your soft and hard spaces and can release energy long past needed to make room for renewing energy. I hope that you discover inhabiting your body is a delicious experience beyond compare.

Negativity and other self-critical comments, which tend to get in the way, are unwelcome. Ask any unhelpful thoughts like "My movement won't be good enough" or "I'm not feeling motivated" or "My writing will be crap" to leave the room. Say goodbye to them and hello to your body. The time set aside for attending to your body is a sacred exploration that flourishes in a supportive environment. Welcome your entry. Welcome your body. Welcome motion, stillness, silence, and words.

1

The Subjective Body

My body. Your body. Our body. Any body.

This fleshy form that accompanies us from birth to death is an amazing source of joy, grief, knowing, and discovery. Month after month and year after year it changes size, shape, and strength. Experiences good and bad leave their mark. Every day it craves food, drink, and sleep. Every day it senses the environment and grapples with making meaning. This fleshy form is also a source of debate about which behaviors and ideas are deemed most appropriate, hygienic, healthy, attractive, productive, and beneficial. Some decrees come from a collective of deciders with whom we may never meet. Other decrees are concocted alone, perhaps in the solitude of home or during a long walk.

You have a body. You are a body. Your body is you. To a degree, you are in control of this body that is you. Some days your body feels good, some days less than good. My body, you say with a radiant smile, is feeling great. Or your shoulders pinched forward, eyes watery and dull, you say, I am not feeling well.

Who is this I? Is this I the same I that eats breakfast and parallel parks without bumping the adjacent car? Is this an I who listens to news or blocks it out? Does this I feel fulfilled no matter what happens or does it struggle with anxiety? Does this I dance or write or recognize the power of each breath?

Is the I separate from the body? We may believe we own our body in a similar way that a car registration delineates ownership. We may believe a social security number establishes this I as a sole non-transferable proprietor. We may believe the body is the hardware and our mind the software which idles each night during sleep.

Words and phrasing have a way of influencing perception. They project an idea that impresses itself upon thought. Words succeed in directing attention. It's impossible, for instance, not to imagine a six toed black cat even if I say not to. Don't imagine it. Try not to.

Too late. The words already shaped perception, already set an impression into motion. The same is true with common understandings of body, many of them derived from philosophers, anthropologists, medical professionals, and clergy among others whose definitions have widespread repercussions.

We can pretty much agree on one premise: we are bodied, that is, you have, or are, a body. Were it otherwise, you would be incapable of reading these words.

Thanks to Descartes and the Age of Enlightenment, references to the body often imply what the body is not. The body is not the mind. Nor is the body the spirit. Mind and spirit are separate from the body. The body is considered our physical form. Cartesian thought recognizes no overlaps among the parts. With this paradigm, we come to know our body largely through science, an outsider's perspective. Observing ourselves from the outside is a perspective that relies on objectivity. The body is an observable object which can be analyzed and measured, all of which leads to commonly accepted truths and valuable information. This perspective informs fields like medicine, physiology, and anatomy.

In these pages, the word "body" is used with broad implications, as syncretic, integrative, holistic, and most importantly, somatic. These pages invite you to experience your personal body and find your way, accompanied by the ideas of each chapter and the exercises located at the end of each chapter, all meant to connect to the vast and amazing resource that is You. Unlike the Cartesian body, the somatic body is all inclusive and emphasizes subjectivity. The somatic body relies on a first person perspective as the source of knowledge and information about our personal body. It recognizes that our physical form overlaps with mind and spirit. The somatic body

Reaching out as a way to reach within

doesn't exclude information that comes from the objective perspective of science but recognizes that full bodily knowing takes place through a combination of objectivity and subjectivity, the latter relying on techniques that inform and reinforce subjectivity. The somatic body acknowledges that the personal subjective body has a highly valuable intelligence of its own—if we access it. The somatic body is a base of knowledge with its own evolutionary intelligence and source of learning and transformation. The somatic body relies on embodiment.

That access comes from somatic practice. Thomas Hanna, the founder of somatics, considers somatics "the body as perceived from within."[1] He defines somatics as a path of "insight, methodology, and understanding"[2] of the body that is knowable primarily through individually lived experienced. The perspective is an inside looking out. Somatic practice is a process of inquiry into how consciousness inhabits the body.

Somatic knowing comes not from any book or movie, not from your grandmother or best friend, but from our own personally lived experience. It comes from learning how we show up in our own body, how we walk, stand, dance, sit at the table and get up. It comes from learning how we express joy and sadness, how we shape experience and how experience shapes us. We don't discount other perspectives. In fact we would be foolish to do so. A multiplicity of perspectives is helpful. Hanna recognizes objectivity and subjectivity as coequal. Both provide valuable information. However, with somatics, the personally lived body perspective matters greatly—and is all the more important because so many of us have been poorly trained or not trained at all to tune into its fount of wisdom.

Your matter, your breath, your seeing, your feelings, your movements, your words, your emotions, and your story are essential. To omit them from awareness and knowledge is like trying to understand an apple pie without ever putting a savory forkful into your mouth.

A Personal Body

A somatic perspective recognizes the body as the site where personal and collective experiences meet. It includes our personal sensations, thoughts and emotions as well as the sensations, thoughts and emotions of others, material that is conscious as well as material that is unconscious. It includes our bodily flesh and the flesh of the earth. The scientific perspective tends to ridicule and suspect many of the findings of the subjective somatic perspective which science considers unreliable and unreproducible. Many times, such findings are unreliable and unreproducible, but that is precisely their strength. Personal experience provides a potent, at times unique insight into ourselves and seeds a broad understanding that is constantly undergoing revision and development.

A subjective perspective is based on personal sensing, each one of us in touch with our body, its sensory phenomenon, personal truths, emotions, rationales, dreams and trials. Our perspective is but one truth in a vast field of truths, minuscule when compared to the Earth's population. Yet these personal, lived truths are the very material that informs who we are, who we can become, and gives rise to a powerful body of knowledge. Our perspective, in short, is everything.

Those of us who have experienced bliss, creative flow, or relief from chronic pain know firsthand the mysteries and awesome power of the body. We have learned to attend to the body's signals, to let it reveal its secrets, and to use that feedback. We have learned that we are not only a body moving through space, an isolated vessel, but that we are space, motion, and momentum, that embodied knowing comes from a marriage of subjectivity and objectivity.

Despite a wish otherwise, we are not always in control of our body. The body does not follow our every command. We cannot, for instance, will happiness into existence. We cannot banish pain at the moment of our wishing it gone. Creative ideas do not show up when we request them to arrive. Our ego is not always in the driver's seat; other factors are also in play.

Life can be inexplicable, contradictory, and confusing. It is also richly complex, dynamic, and exquisite. We are moved by experience, but don't know why. The thunder rattling the windows of our house frightens but also excites us. We break up with a partner, then send a tender text message. Ideas chase after meaning. Meaning chases after experience. Meaning can be slippery and not readily apparent. Emotion clouds thinking. Try as we may, words which we rely on for making life comprehensible sometimes only approximate meaning. Says poet Octavio Paz, "Our senses, our instincts, our imagination are always a step ahead of our reason."[3]

Which is why there's a need for somatics. To get in step with our unique perspective. To touch into our complex, contradictory, and exquisite body. To see around corners and forge new connections. To engage the mystery of our flesh entwined with mind and spirit. To sense and learn, establish personal and interpersonal balance, and become the best of who we are.

Which is why combining somatic awareness with moving and writing is so powerful.

Somatic awareness gets us to refine focus, to tune our attention sharper or closer or wider, to hone in through a specific lens. It gets us to tend to what we hadn't known existed, to revise our relationship to our sensory-motor skills, and entertain new perceptions. Says Hanna,

> It is only through the exclusionary function of awareness that the *involuntary* is made *voluntary*, the *unknown* is made *known,* and the *never-done* is made *doable*. Awareness serves as a probe, recruiting new material for the repertoire of voluntary consciousness. The upshot of this is that somatic learning begins by focusing awareness on the unknown.[4]

As the site where we witness life up close, where we move and are moved, where we are intimate with cellular change, transformation taking place with every breath, thought, and motion, the somatic body is the gateway to creative expression, insight, innate wisdom, intuition, inspiration, innovative thinking, and healing. An intimate knowing of our somatic body leads to self knowing, ease, embodiment, and unimagined openings. The somatic body is an informed body that leads to embodied cognition, creativity, and the path to its own freedom.

Somatic Illiteracy

Yet many of us are somatically uninformed and disembodied. As a character is one of James Joyce's short stories says, "Mr. Duffy lived a few inches from his body."[5] We may know the address for our body, but are unfamiliar with our contents. We recognize ourselves in the mirror, an external viewing, but may not identify or understand our expression, our stiffness, or why we move or feel the way we do. We are only superficially acquainted with the myriad happenings of our body as it changes positions, emotions, and temperature, our homeostasis easily thrown off. We are oblivious to the imprints left by our earliest emotional experiences. Awareness of the multitude of nuanced bodily phenomenon escapes detection. We may be unsure what energizes or de-energizes us, what supports or diminishes well-being, how to relieve tension or how to lift an arm or box without strain, and how to decipher emotions for information and not let them use us. We don't know where we reside along the continuum of aliveness and fatigue nor how to slide the lever toward balance and greater fulfillment. Oblivious to the constant stream of feedback the body provides, we may be unsure how to interpret its many noticeable cues, our somatic intelligence untapped. Essentially, aside from basic bodily functions, we may know little about the range of breath, motion, emotion, and imaginings of our personal body. An incredible resource right at our fingertips is usually underutilized and underappreciated.

This inability to notice and read bodily cues is somatic illiteracy. Somatic illiteracy results from schooling, religion, and other institutions that exclude teaching and supporting kinesthetic, somatic, and emotional intelligence. With limited understanding of the value of somatics, these institutions either fail to recognize or outright demean somatic intelligence, our SIQ, in the same way that they often belittle emotional intelligence. The body, they believe, is justifiably ignorable, the skills and abilities that come from somatic literacy underappreciated. Despite its ability to inform us about our personal body, dance is typically excluded from school as a non-essential extracurricular activity that takes valuable time away from the only subjects deemed necessary such as science, history, and math. Students caught in introspection, a quality essential to increasing SIQ, are mistakenly accused of not paying attention, an outward focus applauded over an inward one. In addition, many religions teach us to ignore and suspect the body, its desires deemed to lead to a host of dark and sinful involvements. Sports welcomes a focus on the body but holds competition as its primary purpose, failing to recognize the benefits of somatic intelligence despite its ability to provide players with greater agility, a result I witness frequently in athletes in my classes who report increased effectiveness at their games.

Developing somatic literacy: Fieval Nihm

The body, too many of us conclude, is not wholly good. Ours, we concede with a downcast gaze and muted voice, is certainly not good enough, not as is. This derogatory attitude contributes to developing a distant, skewed, depersonalized and unhelpful relationship to our flesh. The distance ignites a firestorm of personal denigration. We criticize our flesh, the fault finding endless: we are too fat, too skinny, too weak, too short, too smart, not smart enough, too sensitive, too insensitive. The barrage of negative assessment sentences us to unsuccessful diets, empty work out routines, depression, anxiety, pill taking, excessive alcohol consumption, aggrandizement, and other destructive reactions. We yearn to escape from the unease of our broken relationship, yet don't know how, so we grab at anything that holds even a slight promise of relief. Too often, however, the grab is a superficial and temporary fix, not a lifestyle or attitude change that is required to repair the relationship to our body. The unfortunate result: We disembody and numb out. We are reactive, not responsive. Ignorant to the somatic support available, unwittingly we partake in our demise, alienation from our body contributing to an epidemic of misery, anger, and fear.

Our flesh matters. It matters greatly. It is the conduit to knowledge, creativity, inspiration, and fulfilment. It is the site where all life takes place. It is the site where motions and emotions take place, helping us navigate relating to external events and people. Yet we look away. We look outward for information and affirmation, steering away from listening to and learning about the amazing resource that is our personal body. The signals the body sends out, if we notice them, we don't know how to interpret. Add to this picture daily stressors and the body withdraws further, closed to experience and the present moment, unsure about which people and which activities are trustworthy.

We get stuck, stiff, anxious, numb, pained. The muscles in our back seize up. We have difficulty concentrating. Joy evaporates. We don't know what to do or how to be or feel to resume that much wanted vitality. Or we operate solely out of obligation and routine, another sort of dulling. The mind may make suggestions, but with no way to work with the body, the sought after results of calm, focus, relief, and inspiration may take overlong to arrive.

When I suggest changes to my students and clients to familiarize themselves with the matters of their flesh, they initially balk, uninterested in revising their relationship to their body. They don't want to be considered selfish, somehow considered an indication of depravity. How is self-care which includes expression, balanced nutrition, positive thoughts, self-compassion, exercise and body awareness selfish? Self-care serves as a reminder that we matter, neither one of us more important than the other. Self-care means I can be of utmost benefit to another when I also attend to the well-being of myself. Self-care establishes compassion toward self alongside empathy with others. Yet without somatic intelligence and embodied awareness, we don't know what genuinely contributes to our well-being nor can we locate the line between narcissistic self-involvement and healthy attention. The bitter pill appears no different from the one that rejuvenates.

We ignore body signals at our own peril. Rather than a passing event, pain and suffering becomes constant. We subject ourselves to a vacancy of the body and poverty of the imagination, vulnerable to the pawning and manipulation of others. We render ourselves powerless and reactive, blaming others for our misfortune. Lost is the ability to achieve or maintain balance. Lost is the ability to feel compassion or empathy. Lost is the ability to connect to strengths. Having given up our power, we believe we have few or no choices. Caught in a maze of thoughts and bumped by feelings, the choices we do make may be ineffectual or harmful. The path to fulfillment, we believe, is littered with endless, insurmountable obstacles. Not only do we disconnect from ourselves, but we similarly cut ourselves off from family, friends, and community.

The symptoms of disembodiment are many, unease, confusion, anxiety, and numbness among them. The sensations, feelings, and stories housed in our body which are key to our liberation remain hidden and seemingly inaccessible. With the body closed, so too follows the mind.

The life force, so vital to thriving, we may consider a quaint notion referred to by poets, idealists and others considered hopelessly naive. Perhaps we experienced irrepressible joy in childhood, gleefully jumping into any available puddle, but the joy got ditched along the route to adulthood. Or we had a tumultuous childhood and became stuck in defensive patterns, pulling in, grasping, pushing away, unable to let go. To compensate for absent or weak vitality, we try to manipulate circumstances. We chase after control. We grasp. We hide from ourselves and from others. We make poor choices. At best, we shortchange ourselves; at worst we suffer—continuously.

Admittedly, the image painted here is bleak. I am continually dismayed by the signs of disembodiment in many of my students who struggle with social anxiety, insomnia, eating disorders, shortness of breath, migraines, and low self-worth, among other conditions. I see clients as young as teenagers who have lost their footing from the pressures of society and an unsupportive home environment. Where are moment to moment, genuine satisfaction, generosity, glee, ease, and the ability to be creative?

Despite being a straight-A student, Charlotte found little in her life to celebrate. Her body was contracted, her shoulders rounded, head tilting down. She shriveled further with any encounter with people. She often missed class due to debilitating stomach aches, uncontrollable sweating, and migraines. When I asked how she felt physically or emotionally, she shrugged her shoulders and avoided eye contact. "Where do you feel your head throb," I asked. "Is your stomach pain on the left or right?" After considering my questions, she replied, "I don't know. Everywhere there's pain," she replied, her hand in a languid sweep of her head and torso. When I suggested a few simple movements with deep breaths, she refused to inflate her already drooping body.

Now for the good news. Fortunately, all is not lost, this book devoted to establishing a welcome home in your body regardless of your situation and who you are. The symptoms of Charlotte or anyone else who is disembodied are not terminal. Such symptoms are temporary obstacles only, indicators of changing behavior wanting to take place. They're personal clues and the very signposts on the path to self-knowing. They're the breadcrumbs that lead to embodiment, but only if we take them as opportunities to open up and wake up. The process of coming home to the body and embodying oneself starts as soon as we say Yes to a somatic practice and Yes to the great matter of our flesh.

After only two weeks of attending my class, Maggie announced that the somatic lessons were saving her college career previously threatened by uncontrollable stress. Once she identified the cause of her stress and tracked how it manifested, she discovered new movement and implemented a few necessary changes. Relief came immediately. Her process of somatic awakening had begun. *(Exercise 1:1 Defining the Body)*

Somatic Openings

For somatic awakening to occur, what is needed is shifting awareness to the inner world of the personal living body. Casual attention is replaced by deep listening. Deep listening requires attentiveness with heart, mind, and all the senses. Deep listening establishes us as witness to heart, mind, gut, and sensory stimuli. Deep listening gets us to discern the difference between perceiving stimuli and reactions brought on by the present moment and those rooted in the past. Deep listening invites curiosity into both the conspicuous and subtle phenomena of our body. With deep listening, we suspend judgement on what is noticed. Instead with neutrality, the focus is on what is noticed. Just witness. Pain in the belly? What does it feel like? Heat at the neck? Clenched jaw? A jumble of fragmented thoughts about work? A hollowness at the heart? There is no need to resist or hold back from thoughts, emotions and sensations. If there is resistance, notice that too. Notice how you judge what you notice and where the judgement is felt in your body. Notice what you notice and how you notice it. What is its shape, color, gesture, sound, or any other outstanding feature? The body is invited to be at ease to release, to melt, to reboot, to do whatever it does on its own without our interference.

Deep listening makes known the hidden workings of the body. Something within us stirs, the body and mind awakening from torpor into alertness. We attend to the rise and fall of sensation, the stiffness or pliancy of motion, the stop or flow of emotion, and the way thought and imagination manifests. The hidden peers out from within folds of flesh as a fleeting gesture or flash of feeling. The unconscious scratches at the surface in attempt to be made conscious. Valuable information is contained in what was previously ignored or off limits. We begin to learn how we are more than our habits and more than our reactions.

Once in touch with the body, connections are revealed. We learn to respond rather than react. Choices show up. The path to embodiment, knowing, inspiration, fulfillment, and creative expression are available to anyone who tunes in to the somatic body.

Somatic awakening opens us to feeling, sensing, and taking action. It allows us to abandon old ways of behaving that may be outdated or no longer in our best interest and to adopt new ways more aligned with personal values and well-being. A body in touch with its own being is alive to the moment and open to shedding old skin for new, aware, too, that such shedding, a dynamic process of our aliveness, is taking place subcutaneously regardless of our approval.

Deep listening for a somatic opening: Yoa Thompson

A single decision to turn attention inward is all that is needed to usher in the start of change. The decision prompts a somatic opening and a series of events that forever changes how we live in our body. The change is substantial, an embodied paradigm shift that alters presence and perception. We may walk taller, sleep more deeply, breathe with greater ease, converse more readily with others, while noticing details of our body and surroundings that previously went undetected. A somatic opening is a disruption in how our body usually functions and may occur as a result of happenstance or deliberate action. *(Exercise 1:2 Simple Presence)*

A powerful somatic opening took place for me when I signed up in college for a Movement Improvisation class. Because of my scoliosis, my doctor was opposed to me engaging in movement. When I finally stepped onto the dance floor against his recommendation after years of wearing an invisible brace, my body rigid to avoid an actual brace, my muscles softened one by one. It was as if the windows and doors of the shuttered house of my body flew open. New movement patterns widened the space between my shoulders. My spine flexed and strengthened. Energizing breath filled the cavity of my torso as I embraced a host of movements previously unavailable. My relationship to my body was changing.

I hadn't realized to what degree I had been living disembodied, distant from the world, numb to sensations other than back pain. Prior to class, it had been like watching the world from a couch, my home surrounded by an unbreachable moat that kept me living primarily from my thoughts, not my flesh. With my feet and arms pressing against the floor and my back bending in ways it hadn't in years, my body awakened from dormancy. The world, in turn, greeted me. As strength and flexibility increased, so, too, connections with emotions, sensations, dreams, friends, family, studies, and a new found devotion to dance and to the process of somatic awakening. My somatic opening birthed a curiosity about the body, dance, and somatics, the doors of perceptions flung wide open.[6]

I witnessed a similar birth with Maggie and with Charlotte when they finally agreed to deepen their breath and tend to their body with more care. Letting go of habitual patterns tied to stress gave them more energy. Their openness to their body made all the difference.

The body, mind, and spirit work together. They collaborate, share, collude. They fuss and inform, tire and inspire, stand up to and release themselves from needless clutches. The entwining is not static but dynamic, a cornucopia of embodying in constant motion. Each moment, the nerves, musculature, fascia, and cells dance with the current of life. Each moment we breathe in the world and the world flushes us with its ever changing conditions. We cannot step into the same river of our body twice.

The body is more than our physical form. Yes, the body is skin, bones, blood, and organs, but the body is also breath, water, air, and energy. It is hormones, neural firing, and cellular respiration. It is how we see, touch, smell, hear, move, sense, think, imagine, and make meaning. It is our attention, intention, and inattention, our delight and anger, our work and play. At times, what takes place such as the ouch from a burn is easily graspable. Other times, it is elusive and mysterious such as a belly flutter, a whoosh in the ears, or a phantasmal image that arrives from a dreamlike state.

There is no on-off switch to somatic awakening. We may be graced with an initiating somatic opening but then must decide to pursue an ongoing somatic practice and practice awareness. A practice of awareness is easy enough: this moment, then next; this flinch, then yawn, then abdominal contraction, then memory of yesterday's swim, then blink, then hearing a car pass, then glancing at our coffee cup on the desk and so on. A conclusion reached yesterday may not apply now. Or tomorrow. Every moment offers new material and with our body sensitizing to such changes, it's up to us to notice what's different. Somatic awareness gets us observing those details and adapting as needed.

Embodiment and the Power of Connection

Turning attention inward to the somatic self is a transformative act. Attention changes mind. Attention changes body. Attention changes energy. Attention alters neural pathways and enriches the imagination. Attention directs the currents of the body toward embodiment. Embodiment gets us to feel and know more of who we are and to recognize possibilities and exercise choice.

Notice. That's all. Our body is communicating. Always. It's up to us to deeply listen and open to each moment.

The body is amazingly intelligent. It continually self regulates, sustaining numerous physiological systems, ensuring oxygen, blood, hormones, and cells function as intended. It continually communicates its condition, its wants and needs, its reactions and understanding. The body is a symphony of vital information that welcomes turning our mind, heart, and gut toward what matters. We observe. We attend with curiosity. We say hello to our flesh.

Ironically, the more we investigate and engage a physical inquiry into our personal body, the more we connect with universal truths. The particulars of our body lead to a larger body of knowledge, to wisdom itself. In studying oneself, we change the self. In connecting to ourselves, we connect to others. We engage in a somatic practice to improve upon our personal conditions and end up improving conditions for much more.

Experiencing connections leads us to inhabit the entirety of our body, skin, breath, and bone, our motion and emotion, the thoughts and feeling connected to the flesh of our body and those overlapping with other bodies. We learn to recognize the difference between deceit and truth because we acquire the skill to read bodily clues. We know how to plug into flow and when to honor limitations. We learn to recognize and welcome the life pulse, that vital current of subtle energy coursing through us, and make decisions based on what supports our well-being. We learn to use emotions to make informed choices. Our daily practice consists of feeling into and supporting body, mind, breath, energy, and imagination. Our daily practice consists of connecting to our life pulse and letting it guide us to the heights of our potential.

Somatic awareness is accessible to anyone who turns their attention toward it. Somatic awareness means tuning into sensations, emotions, images, movement, and imagination. We uncover the memories stored in the connective tissue of our being. We develop somatic intelligence and a personal body vocabulary. We practice being a body, not just any body, but our personal play by play, moment to moment, sensing, feeling, moving body. By embodying the flesh of our being, we come to know our body and practice our personally expressive aliveness.

We discover how the movement and rigidity of our body reflects the movement and rigidity of our mind. We discover how intention leads attention, how the contents of thought reciprocally influences energy, and how embodied connections lead to choices that support our highest purpose.

We may try to control the body with the mind but quickly find the body rebels and refuses to comply. Consider the difficulty in starting and sticking to a diet or getting up from the couch to complete a chore and doing so with cheer. A better arrangement is discovering and supporting the inherent ways the mind and body collaborate on delivering the wholeness of who we are and working with, not against our rhythms. This wholeness provides a much broader definition than either the body or the mind alone can supply.

Embodiment reinforces rooting in the power of presence,

Practicing presence with an outward gaze in nature: Fieval Nihm

awareness situated in the present moment, and engaging the awesome mystery of life. Awareness of the present moment filters out the static and distractions that disrupts presence. Presence allows us to drop identification with the stories and feelings that imprison us and position us in alliance with a more central, fluid power. Presence allows us to sever ties that hold us to any obstacles stemming from the past and to be available to the current of life giving energy. Embodiment supports presence and being responsive to the ever changing conditions of now. This awareness can only be practiced in the now. This moment, then what follows, another moment, then another is the very doorway to ease and freedom.

We can't notice every bit of stimuli since at any given moment, given that billions of macro and micro activities are taking place within our body and in close proximity constantly. But we may notice tension in our shoulder. We may notice our position and what part of our body touches the seat and the floor, how our shirt grazes our arms, whether our jaw is slack or closed, how the waist band of our pants presses against our belly. We can notice the colors of the walls, the blaring horn, the bright overhead light, the waft of coffee from next door. We can notice shame or delight. When we engage in somatic awareness, we notice details of our body and surroundings that previously escaped detection because we were preoccupied. What's important is not creating an exhaustive list of stimuli, but noticing what you notice and eventually recognizing which stimuli form patterns and which are isolated events. *(Exercise 1:3 Quick Inventory)*

Presence allows the body to inhale and exhale without effort. It welcomes creative expression and wisdom. Presence works hand in hand with the life pulse with its own rhythm and timing which may not accord with our preferences, but ultimately works in our behalf. All we need to do is show up.

Somatic Paths

In the last several decades, more and more somatic techniques have been developed and utilized across many disciplines for a technique's ability to increase strength, flexibility, insight, expression, health, innovation, and overall well-being. The growing use of somatic techniques is helped along by, among other factors, the shortcomings of the traditional medical establishment with its emphasis on pharmacological solutions, an inadequate education system biased toward rote learning of objective information, and the increasing popularity of meditation and mindfulness techniques whose effectiveness is increasingly backed by neurological research. Additionally, more and more psychologists such as Pat Ogden, who developed sensorimotor psychotherapy, use somatic techniques in the understanding and treatment of post-traumatic stress and other mental health disorders. Life coaches, too, are finding wide applicability with clients navigating the challenges of creating a home and work life balance. The result: the somatic field is demonstrating ample signs of growth.

Each somatic technique has a particular focus that typically arises out of the background and needs of its founder. The focus may be fascia unwinding, skeletal alignment, cerebrospinal fluids, trauma, or energy flow and may be of particular interest to those in fields such as psychology, anatomy, health, dance, athletics, theater, leadership, medicine, health care or anyone looking to raise their somatic intelligence. Dance educator Bonnie Bainbridge Cohen developed Body-Mind-Centering, a program for studying anatomical, physiological, psychophysical and developmental principles using movement, touch, voice and mind. Milton Trager developed Trager Mentastics to release deep habitual movement patterns for ones that support ease of motion. Ron Kurtz developed the Hakomi Method based on his interest in Eastern philosophy, psychotherapeutic technique, and systems theory.

My curiosity led to studying Continuum, Authentic Movement, Process-Oriented Psychology, Alexander Technique, Feldenkrais, yoga, Tai Chi, and Contact Improvisation to name several. Each one increased my sensory perception, creative expression, kinesthetic and proprioceptive intelligence, and touch sensitivity, essentially the particulars of how I dwell in my body. Each technique expanded my somatic understanding, vocabulary, and expression.

For a somatic opening to take place and a practice to be worth its pursuit, it must contain elements of introspection, proprioception, and kinesthesia. Proprioception is the ability to sense the interior environment of the body, specifically its motion and location, in relation to the external environment. Kinesthesia is awareness of the visible motion of the body. Benefit comes from tuning inward and heightening alertness to the numerous sensory stimuli and felt nuances of being taking place. Benefit comes from an awareness of emotions, sensations, and thoughts. A good example is yoga. Its historic origins are very much somatic. Yoga, by definition, is a yoking of mind, body, and spirit, an entwining performed with balance. Yet many current practitioners use the discipline to tone the body while ignoring the broader holistic connections. The appearance of a fit body is considered a kinesthetic accomplishment, but it excludes linking it to the mental and spiritual calisthenics. There's nothing wrong with using yoga this way, although I would argue that it's not yoga, but a type of physical exercise. It's important to recognize the difference between building physical muscles without building the muscles of mind and spirit simultaneously. Even people engaged in a somatic practice and meditation can be disembodied and ignore key parts of themselves. Psychologist John Welwood came up with a term for this ignoring, spiritual bypass, which describes using spiritual ideas and practices of one's tradition to avoid facing unresolved psychological wounds. For many of us, it is too easy to somatically bypass key bodily connections. With somatic bypass, we are similarly avoidant and numb, putting on a superficial happy face and body while ignoring sensations and emotions that may be uncomfortable but ultimately lead to genuine growth and balance.

This is where a regular somatic practice helps. It gets us to pay attention, to look anew and touch the truths of this moment. It gets us to notice what we are sensing and feeling and, equally important, to notice when we are withdrawing, hiding, and numbing out, our ears, eyes, and mind closed to what our body is trying to tell us. *(Exercise 1:4 A Moment's Notice)*

Resonant Writing as Somatic Path

The somatic technique explained in this book relies on the synergy of combining moving with writing and deep listening. This potent blend opens pathways for creative expression, embodied knowing, healing, and integrative being. The act of moving furthers the articulation derived from writing just as the act of writing furthers the articulation derived from moving. Resonant writing generates a rich investigation and expression of personal experience and understanding profoundly grounded in the body. The technique teaches us to read our nonverbal and verbal bodily manifestations and to increase awareness, which shifts sensory sensitivity and revises how we show up in and think about our personal body. The technique leads to discovering the value of our personally embodied truths and how they contribute to fulfillment and achievement of our highest aims. We take up residence within ourselves, in the flesh of embodied knowing, and discover the profound difference between knowing with the head and knowing with our full being.

We move from sensation. We feel from moving. We write from moving. We move and write with being. The practice alters how we experience our body, what we perceive, and what we recognize as possible. We take up residence in the house that is our body and feel at home, full of relief and renewal.

Combining moving with writing and deep listening engenders neural integration, areas of the brain brought into coherence, strengthening synaptic connections and establishing new pathways. The combination leads to significant increases in somatic and mental intelligence. It leads as well to increasing overall intelligence, connections between experience and ideas newly forming.

Here is a laboratory for neuroplasticity, change taking place on fundamental neural levels, from atoms and cells, from the body expressing itself, awareness tugging and shifting the boundary between consciousness and unconsciousness, the separation between body and mind impossible to uphold. Here is a mindfulness technique that emphasizes body awareness and imagination. At every turn of phrase and rise of sensation, the technique activates awareness and reminds us about the nature of our flesh. We embody. We develop great facility in knowing and being, an expanded somatic epistemology placing a more colorful palette of experience and invention at our finger tips, in how we stand, move, interact, meet challenges, and show up with our body each day. We discover the expansiveness of imagination, embodied cognition, a knowing who we are and what we are becoming. Once we have engaged the process, it's hard to go back to who we were. There is instead standing with growing integrity in the truth of our body and the freedom that comes with feeling embodied presence.

The response I hear most from my students and clients who engage in the process is astonishment. "I didn't know my body can move like that," or "I didn't realize I could make my migraine disappear," or "I've never written a poem before," or "I didn't know I knew that." They change their attitude, posture, how they do their job, how they interact with a partner, and how they use creative expression. They speak up when a situation calls for more volume and listen more attentively to subtle cues. They find the rhythms of moving and writing inform them about their lives.

The body senses and knows more than we give it credit for, its wisdom arising when obstructions are removed, when we connect to the inherent rhythms of our body. What appears is a different way of knowing, an increased range of motion, deeper breath, ease, a sense of spaciousness, connective tissue hydrating and renewing, new definitions and articulations of flesh and word opening portals to the previously unimagined.

Movement by itself is a powerful activity. It is a precursor to conceptualizing which tends to remove and abstract us from feeling. Movement roots us in our body and the flesh of experience. Movement may be the closest we get to expressing the immediacy of the lived, felt body. "Movement," says choreographer Martha Graham, "never lies."[7] The body is always in motion in visible and less visible ways. Blood continually travels arterial highways and cells continually respire. Skin and muscle expand, contract, push, take weight. Movement engages the connective tissue system, the collagen fibers that extend throughout the body from the outermost layer of skin to the interior of cells. Connective tissue is piezoelectric, transmitting electricity, the potency of those currents increasing with movement. Movement puts us in touch with our body and every rock, stairwell, floor and person that we encounter.

Writing by itself is also a powerful activity. Writing expresses and verbally defines an otherwise amorphous, fleeting experience. It matters not whether we use a conventional or unconventional narrative, use pencil to meander across a page or stick to lines and type. Words contain the history of a culture. How we use those words gets us participating in the making of culture and ourselves.

Writing creates order. Writing defines experience, furthers thought, and contributes to making sense of a passing experience that may otherwise seem chaotic, contradictory, negligible, or overwhelming. Writing makes us intelligible and generates a product that makes later reflection possible.

Somatic awareness lets us come to know the body at rest and in action. We need not be doing anything special. Both lounging on a chair, feet up, torso in recline or sprinting across gravel, fists punching the air, sweat dripping all provide valuable clues about our body. Somatic awareness gets us to see how we show up in our body each moment, tight or relaxed, numb or enlivened, and to what degree we feel in or out of kilter, disjointed or coherent.

Applying somatic awareness to writing shows the intimate link and resonance between words and our body. It's a two way street. Our storied verbal expression shapes our body. Conversely our body influences the choice and manner of our words. Words help to define our body and our body, in turn, influences our choice of words. What we tell and how we language ourselves determines the words and ideas that flock to us. Writing in conjunction with somatic awareness can also liberate us, shifting the way we experience and define ourselves, leading the way to insight and expression. Applying somatic awareness to writing awakens us to the power of these verbal messengers. Recognizing the two-way direction and impact of words trafficking with body allows an active and informed participation in the exchange. We discover how words matter because we find how they inhabit and shape us. They lead to new territory or impede us. They stop us with each pronouncement or guide us around obstacles. When we apply somatic awareness to writing, all roads lead to other roads, the body pliant and present, words responsive and lively, all working hand in hand, step after step, our gaze tied to the belly or the heaven of our balance. Words open us to worlds as does motion and somatic awareness. *(Exercise 1:5 Resonant Words)*

I am not advocating that we move at the same time as we write, one hand on the page, the other extending into the nearby space. Perhaps the most dexterous among us can carry off this bipartite activity without a bruise, but this is not the purpose of this technique. Moving and writing with somatic awareness takes place sequentially. Move, then write. Or write, then move. In this way each inform, compel, and further the other and heightens overall awareness, perception, and connections. It brings verbal and nonverbal expression into greater congruence. We not only come home to ourselves, but settle in with a sensitivity to the position and layout of every verbal and nonverbal gesture.

We initiate an experience with the body and words with integrity, deep listening, and openness. Expectation is dropped. Curiosity awakens. Movement moves us. Words move us. The writing writes us, telling our story or a new story. We watch and listen and feel. We breath in synch with the expressive depths of being. The body shares its experience and wisdom, its knowing, feeling, and guiding. But only if we pay attention, only if we let it inform us, and let it lead to the unknown.

Some Specifics

What follows is a brief overview of this technique. The ideas will be elaborated upon in subsequent pages along with accompanying exercises to provide you experience. The ingredients are not intended to be done in the order they appear, but are listed to show the components that define the process. Modify them as seems necessary. Use them to engage the energy of your personal path, to embody yourself and become informed about your flesh.

- *Write intention.* Jot down your intention at the start of each session to set focus. *(Exercise 1:6 Intentions)*
- *Ground.* Align your body with the earth.
- *Center.* Establish balance of emotional, psychological and physical systems. Find a flexible, internal neutral space.
- *Be still.* Stillness promotes raising awareness of somatic events already taking place and becoming aware of micro-events.
- *Move.* Moving which tends to be more deliberate and includes both large and small patterns of motion can enhance awareness.
- *Write.* Write about your experience, write about your body, and write from the body. Write to deepen movement and somatic awareness. Write from several perspectives.

- *Pace.* Write and move with different speeds to allow for varied connections.
- *Notice perceptions.* Attend to each sense and note the channel dominating your perceptions. Notice what takes place when you switch channels.
- *Follow the flow of attention.* Watch your mind, its focus, and the ebb and flow of consciousness.
- *Pursue impulses.* Let go of resistance. Fleeting and lasting impulses are tied to the life pulse and are rich with creative energy and information. This applies to moving, being still, and writing.
- *Alternate.* Alternate between being and doing, actively and passively expressing, guiding and allowing.
- *Witness verbal resonance.* Notice how words and phrases impact your body. Notice the storied areas of your body. Resonance involves assigning a location and quality of movement to abstract ideas and locating where in your body a word, phrase or belief lives.
- *Be physically inquisitive.* Welcome curiosity about ways your body expresses itself.
- *Experiment.* Experiment and improvise with writing. Play with words on the page, in various positions, with different voices, sounds, perspectives, points of view, and meaning. Experiment with moving. Play with space, speed, rhythm, and pattern.
- *Activate imagination.* Deliberately engage the imagination to further the somatic journey.
- *Open to coherence and synergy.* Enter liminal spaces, the gray areas between knowing and not knowing. Find a balance between control and surrender. Notice what shows up.
- *Reflect.* Complete a session by returning to your sensory attention. Notice any shifts, insights, creations. Take a few minutes to ground your energy.

These are the ingredients that will draw you more deeply into yourself. Make them your own. Find out what they mean for you. They are the start for discovering your body as the site of inquiry, perceiving, learning, creating, and understanding. (*1:7 Writing, Moving, and Mindful Awareness*)

Exercises

1:1 Defining the Body

- Consider definitions of the body you were given in school, at home, and elsewhere. Is your definition the same as these? How do you define body?

1. The Subjective Body

Write a definition of the body that is objective and commonly agreed upon. Come up with two more definitions, again based on objective understandings of the body.

- Come up with a subjective definition. Let it reflect your personal life experience. Let your definition be honest, playful, poetic, contradictory, or whatever seems most fitting. Do not limit yourself. As you deliberate and write your definition, note any physical and emotional reactions. Write two more definitions based on criteria from personal experience.
- Put a hand on your belly and ask, "What is this body?" Put a hand on your shoulders, face, heart or anywhere else that invites your hand. How does its placement affect what you feel and think? Write the impressions or emotions that arose with each placement.
- Walk slowly across the room aware that your somatic body is mobilizing through space. As you traverse the room, what new information arises to include in your definitions when you consider your somatic body? Write about that new information.

1:2 Simple Presence

- You are reading these words, perhaps in your home, the library, the subway. Look around. Let your eyes dart about and linger here and there.
- Return your gaze to the page. Notice the position of your hands, the angle of your torso, your jaw, lips, legs and feet. Are you comfortable? If not, what is the location of your discomfort?
- Shift to a more comfortable position. What changed? Did you move your legs, arms, and gaze? Did you take a deeper breath? Find a position that allows you to feel relaxed, you body in alignment, your thoughts settling.

1:3 Quick Inventory

- Quickly write a list of what you are noticing this moment. Write whatever comes into your awareness. Don't think about it. Take no longer than a few minutes. Once complete, read it through. How does taking inventory impact what you notice?
- Take another quick inventory later today or in a few days. Compare the lists. What is new? The same? What patterns do you see?

1:4 A Moment's Notice

- Set a timer for 10 minutes. Jot down the first thing you notice about your surroundings and your body.

- What is the relationship between what you noticed first and what followed? What changed about your body and surroundings?

1:5 Resonant Words

- Get a dictionary or any other book. Randomly open a page and read a phrase. What thought, memory, or sensation is stirred? How does its sound or meaning appeal or offend you? Where in your body does the response originate? What sensations are associated with it?
- Make a list of about 5 words that you like for whatever reason. Make another list of 5 words you don't like. As you write, notice bodily responses to the words.

1:6 Intention

Coming up with an intention is a powerful part of the process of embodying your actions and words. An intention clarifies direction. It is the wind as well as the sails behind a hoped for action. It provides direction and guidance. Coming up with an intention doesn't guarantee it manifests. Other factors like hidden beliefs can be at play as well. But it does clarify thinking, organizes energy, and sets a series of events into motion.

- Write an intention for reading this book.
- Be specific. Take your time to clarify your meaning. Carefully choose your words.
- Be positive. Words have power. They emanate. Phrase yourself positively, for instance, "I want a great outcome" rather than "I want to avoid failure."
- Be realistic. Avoid overreach. Going too far leads to disappointment when you don't meet your mark.
- Be open. Surrender. Let life energy take over.
- Revisit your statement when you finish this book (and at the close of each exercise) to see what took place. Whether you hit the mark or veered off course is helpful information. Hitting the mark is applaudable, but veering off holds its own surprises and may be more valuable than you initially think.

1:7 Writing, Moving, and Mindful Awareness

- Provide an objective definition for "writing," for "moving," and for "mindful awareness."
- Provide a subjective definition for "writing," "moving," and "mindful awareness." Write first thoughts. Base the definitions on personal experience.

- Take a few breaths. Write freely about these ideas and how they impact or don't impact your life. Write from the heart, head, and gut. Keep the writing in flow.
- How do you explain any differences between the objective and subjective definitions of these terms? How might those differences influence your attitude while carrying out these actions?

2

The Perceiving Body

While Tyrell danced in class, I witnessed a brilliant glow emanating from his head and enveloping his body. I have seen this with other students and clients but not so lustrously. His was golden, effervescent, and extended about two feet out from his skin. When I stepped near, tingles like a soft rain left me feeling light and expansive. At the end of class one day, I asked him to stay after.

"Do you know," I began reluctantly, unsure how he would receive the information, "that you're glowing?"

"Yes," he replied, "and so are you."

Needless to say, a lengthy conversation ensued and continued throughout the semester. I learned that eighteen months earlier while playing rugby, Tyrell hit his head on the ground and suffered a severe concussion. His world went black with the exception of a pinhole of light. He could hear but his vision, short-term memory and coordination were gone, knocked to a netherworld. A doctor pronounced the condition permanently hopeless, but his mother wisely consulted a second doctor who suggested acupuncture and yoga which he diligently pursued. The payoff was positive. Tyrell's senses returned but with a significant shift, an increased sensitivity to phenomena. He perceived the arrival of external phenomena first as waves of energy. Once the waves closed in on his body, these waves transformed, close proximity translating them into a sensible language, into voices, images, sensation, emotions, and words. The change from his pre-to post-concussion brain was like lowering a dimmer switch at one lobe and upping it in another, a rewiring of his neural circuitry which led to new sensory awareness and perceptual pathways.

Such awareness and pathways opened long ago for me. My heightened sensory attunement resulted not from an injury but from ongoing practices of dance, writing, and meditation. These practices tuned me in to the keen details of motion, expression, and calm. They dredged material lying distant from awareness into the light. They shifted casual attention into a rich

2. The Perceiving Body

dynamic tapestry of perceptions. Each practice prompts one area of the brain to go offline temporarily, another to turn on, multiple areas in a heated exchange. Neurologists using PET scans to monitor activity show different parts of the brain lighting up depending on our sensory engagement. Among their findings, they conclude that dance strengthens neuronal connections and memory.[1] They show that writing stimulates cells in the frontal lobe, the reticular activating system, and that hand writing, as opposed to typing, gets us paying greater attention to details. Meditation done with somatic awareness slows down the parietal lobe, beta waves decreasing, allowing not only deep relaxation, but lasting brain changes which we experience as enhanced sensory awareness.[2] Says neuroscientist Sara Lazar, "[L]ong-term meditators have an increased amount of gray matter in the insula and sensory regions, the auditory and sensory cortex. Which makes sense. When you're mindful, you're paying attention to your breathing and to sounds, the present moment experience, and shutting cognition down. It stands to reason your senses would be enhanced."[3]

The deliberate connecting of mind with body, language with perceptions, and sensation with emotion leads the way to strengthening connections

Perceiving internal and external space: left to right, top to bottom; Yao Thompson, John Swift, Aaron Brown, Cheryl Pallant, Amy Impellizzeri, Celina Alvarez, Robbie Kinter, Fieval Nihm

between otherwise isolated parts, an active coherence that expands consciousness and opens doors to enhanced experience, creativity and insight. Writing about his experiences and dancing led Tyrell to better understood what he was perceiving.

We write to express and find out what we know. We move to express and find out what we know. Together they give voice and form to impressions and further expression and knowing. Mind and body, language and emotion each enhance and deeply connect to each other. Our physicality, knowing, and creativity are deeply entwined. Actively pursuing their connectivity and engaging ourselves somatically serves in strengthening sensitivity and consciousness, developing senses, shifting behavior, and opening us to new perceptions.

My involvement with movement and writing over the years provided ample evidence that expanded my perceptions. I feel enlivened, awake, in a gratifyingly intimate dance with the universe, all of which keeps me returning again and again to these practices. When I dance, my body becomes alert yet calm, strong yet soft. Time seems to slow even if my exertion is lengthy and the movements complex. Contrary as this sounds, this slowing allows for lightening-quick responses to actions that, with less awareness, could result in a bruising stumble. For instance, when sliding off a partner's shoulder, my arms and torso both relax and firm to handle the encounter of the floor. My external focus, the peripheral awareness that every dance practitioner learns, extends feet away from me to avoid knocking into someone or something. My focus is internal as well, my proprioceptive awareness constantly adapting to changes. Athletes talk about a similar principle, their reaction time, by necessity, immediate. They cannot afford to pause and ponder the situation, but must optimize the ball or player or space on the field with a quick reaction. To do otherwise is to miss an opportunity.

Writing, too, provides ample evidence about myself. Phrases aided me in focusing upon sensory events that might have otherwise slipped from notice and memory. Writing became a way to define experience, to pause long enough to turn fleeting phenomena over in my mind, to develop material that otherwise quickly gets absorbed into the flesh of our being. Writing gets us to check for veracity, to express what hasn't been expressed. The writing allows us to process what has taken place and shift what we recognize as possible. Tyrell sought fitting words to match his unfamiliar experience. Previous writing had been linear and precise but as he wrote about his perceptions, he surprised himself by writing poetry full of sonic elements, his lines loose and rhythmic. His writing felt more authentic than previous trials. It also provided an understanding about the changes taking place in his perceptual world.

2. The Perceiving Body

Dance reframes the world, how we inhabit it, and how we inhabit the body. The same holds true for writing. Both stir belief systems, our center of gravity, and responses to circumstances. They alter visceral engagement with stimuli. Every one of our actions sets off a chain reaction of reactions and responses. Slowing down to engage in a somatic practice gets us to loosen our usual habits and see details otherwise ignored.

A reaction tends to be instantaneous. A hidden momentum takes over. A stimulus is presented and we swiftly react, often without any reflection. A response involves contemplation. We observe it for the emotions and beliefs driving it. We listen deeply to better understand the phenomenon of the body and what choices may exist. Both give us information about ourselves and our situation.

The multifarious phenomena of the body, whether they occur while moving, writing, or carrying out something more ordinary like pulling weeds is a type of choreography. The multifarious phenomena is also a sibilant stanzaed poem, every word falling into a space on the page, each turn of phrase pointing toward meaning and setting expression free. The phenomenon of the body is also a collection of stories with a motley assembly of characters and scenes drawn from loss and love and awe. Every moment supplies diverse and amazing bodily events awaiting the audience of our attention.

Turning our attention and somatically attuning is a voluntary act. How well we do so is determined by practice. The muscle of our attention strengthens with use and is available to anyone who says Yes to the process. That turning and attuning strengthens abilities often taken for granted.

We believe we are passively receiving stimuli from our environment. When we settle the thoughts, emotions and motions of our body, we can identify the phenomenon enveloping and acting upon us and find out otherwise. We find, too, how to actively engage with that information and decide which we detect and which we allow as influence.

The Senses

To perceive the world around us, traditional biology points to our five primary senses, sight, smell, hearing, taste, and touch, each linked to a specific organ. This is Perception 101. These five senses carry great responsibility in determining how we come to know ourselves and assist us in navigating the world. Sight and touch, for instance, help us walk through a doorway without hitting the frame. Our ears inform us when our dog is barking at the back door ready to come inside. These are also examples of direct knowing. There is no intermediary, no third party filter telling us what is so. Rather, the information conveyed through our senses tells us what is going on.

Using our senses for knowing seems straight forward enough. Open our eyes and see. Extend our hand and touch. Easy enough, right? Yet it's more complicated. A host of internal and external distractions or perceptual noise clouds our sensing or wipes out a clear signal. An emotional state, stress, a preoccupying thought, pain, and nearby activity are some of the noise that impedes the signal and diverts our attention. If, for instance, we're lingering wistfully on last month's trip to the ocean, we may not see the person right in front of us. If worried about a test, we may not notice our hunger. If busy watching a red Ferrari pull up in front of our house, we may not hear a friend speaking about a visit from an uncle. We project ourselves into another time—last month's easy roll on the floor—or into the future—when we anticipate wearing cotton pants to roll without slipping on the floor. These examples of noise take our attention away from being aware of present sensory stimuli.

At any given moment, there are thousands of sensory events taking place within our body and beyond it that compete for our attention. What about the gurgle in our stomach, the strain in our neck, the tightness in our diaphragm? What about the curl of our friend's hair, the sheen and matching hubcaps on the Ferrari, the hum of a fan? What about the energetic waves emanating from any of it? The avalanche of stimuli is too much for any person to process consciously and remain balanced and focused. It's a wonder that we don't topple over from the regular onslaught.

There's more to seeing than meets the eye, more to feel than touches the skin, and more ways to categorize perceiving than the classical model of the five senses. Interestingly, which model we apply and how we use it significantly influences what we detect and what we believe is detectable.

Heightened sensitivity is among my more noticeable recent developments. I hear faint nearby sounds as well as those from a distance, sounds that companions beside me don't hear at all. A tiny stone on the dance floor under my foot sends a sharp shooting pain as if a cut from a knife. Without seeing facial or any other visible cues, I pick up another's emotion and thoughts. I vibrate from written and spoken words and can locate where they land in or launch from my body. I detect micro-movements in my back, neck, belly and elsewhere. I watch how stress, diverse in its manifestations, chooses to appear one time as forgetfulness, the next time as a contraction deep in my sacrum. I have witnessed sensation reveal its tie to events long dismissed from mind, events bubbling to the surface and new understanding. I've been fortunate to make use of this sensitivity. It comes in handy in working with students and clients who I lead to developing greater sensitivity and making better sense of their world. Such sensitivity is available to all of us. When we pause our usual ways of perceiving and reactions and take note of what else may be in our surroundings, we discover a world awaiting us.

My client Jen suffered regularly from migraines and didn't know their cause. "They just show up weekly out of the blue," she said. We worked at unfolding her phrase, "out of the blue," finding ways to represent it in movement and then writing about her movements. She discovered she often clenches her jaw which corresponded with critical thoughts about herself. As she became aware of the frequency of these behaviors, she learned to loosen her jaw and express self-compassion. Eventually she found a range of motion and expression that made her feel more at ease and the migraines disappeared. Once she turned her attention, she was able to perceive the information her body was provided.

Education theorist Howard Gardner suggests perceptual ability is largely the result of intelligences, what he also refers to as languages or sensory modalities. His theory of multiple intelligences suggests that our facility with our intelligences determines how and what we perceive. He identifies nine intelligences: verbal–linguistic intelligence (word smart), musical–rhythmic (music smart), visual–spatial (picture smart), logical–mathematical (numbers and reasoning smart), bodily–kinesthetic (body smart), interpersonal (people smart) intrapersonal (self-smart), naturalistic (nature smart) and existential-spiritual (religion smart).[4] Most grade schools rely on verbal-linguistic intelligence and logical–mathematical sensory modalities as a measure of overall intelligence which means that students who test weak in these areas are deemed to be low in intelligence. His model not only points out biases in our school system but also serves as a helpful reminder that there is no singular standard of intelligence.

Gardner's ideas have gained widespread attention, however his is not the only available model as more and more psychologists, education theorists, and business leaders develop ways to define intelligence. A marked difference is apparent in Danah Zohar and Ian Marshall's model which emphasizes spiritual intelligence and is based in psychology and quantum physics. Their model brings out the importance of the transpersonal which they see omitted from other models. Their model is broken down into categories such as vibrational intelligence, cellular intelligence, intuitive intelligence and personal intelligence. They consider spiritual intelligence the ultimate intelligence given its unitive ability. They state that spiritual intelligence "facilitates a dialogue between reason and emotion, between body and mind. It provides a fulcrum for growth and transformation. It provides the self with an active, unifying, meaning given centre."[5]

Regardless of the model, what's clear is that the strength of an intelligence is a combination of inborn ability, schooling and conditioning. We are typically good in one or a few areas and weak in the others. If we have neither been schooled nor have an inborn ability in a weak intelligence, we may never be privy to the stream of information that comes with it, an entire vocabulary and way of perceiving omitted from our perceptual picture. Most of us, for instance, remain incognizant to the positioning of our body and the historical factors that contribute to its shape. Activities contributing to building somatic intelligence are frequently omitted from grade school where students spend hour after hour moored to a chair. It's no wonder so many of us fail to notice otherwise perceivable phenomena such as the slant of our lips or jaw tension. Understandably we may conclude this information is non-existent because rightfully so, based on personal experience, we have no information. We may also conclude that no such information exists for anyone. A more accurate assessment is that it doesn't exist in our perceptual frame.

Adjust the perceptual frame and the world is experienced quite differently. Place greater attention on somatic intelligence, which I go into greater depth here and in the next chapter, and find that heightened attentiveness to the body is foundation to all other intelligences. The body is home base. The body is ground zero. But none of this is apparent if we experience ourselves as an empty vessel controlled by a brain.

Further Intelligence Models

Although this book is very much about reinforcing the value of first hand personal experience, direct knowing as vital to embodied knowing, it is advisable to recognize the likelihood—I'd go so far as to say the inevitability—of blind spots. We never perceive the com-

Perceptual frames alter seeing

plete picture. Despite a longing for surety, our knowing is never one hundred percent. It's not that what we perceive isn't accurate—it may be. It's just that another perspective, one that may challenge our knowing, may also be accurate, an understanding that seems contradictory and impossible. Deep listening with the entire body requires humility and availing ourselves to a technique that opens our senses. *(Exercise 2:1 Primary Senses Sitting Awareness)*

Another wholly different model for perceiving is Process Oriented Psychology, referred to also as Process Work, created by psychologist Arnold Mindell. In *Working on Yourself Alone*, he frames perceptual paths as awareness channels. He identifies six main ones: proprioception (awareness of the body position and interior experiences), visual (awareness of internal and external images), auditory (awareness of speaking, listening, and hearing of inner voices), kinesthetic (awareness of body motion), relationships (awareness of communicating with others), and world (awareness of social issues such as sexism, classism, and environmental issues).[6] Subsequent books further his ideas to include other channels, subchannels, and metachannels.

With Mindell's model, were I to say I'm hungry, that's my proprioceptive channel. Were I to feel ashamed about eating a large portion in front of others, I'm in a relationship channel. If I write about my hunger but glance out the window at a squirrel, I have switched to a visual channel. Mindell recognizes that at any given moment, our attention knowingly occupies a single channel and switches frequently minute to minute. There are two primary levels of what he refers to as "occupying a channel" which has to do with being conscious or unconscious of the channel from which we operate. Usually we passively occupy a channel, that is, we have neither chosen the channel nor realize which channel

Biases color conclusions

we're in. Interestingly, when we decide to switch channels or consciously and actively occupy a channel, new information and perceptions arrive. Additionally, if we dwell in an unfamiliar channel, which for many of us is proprioception, we likely feel disoriented. The less familiar channel challenges our usual way of perceiving while revealing an alternative pathway of sensory awareness. We may experience this alternative pathway as an altered or otherworldly state due to our inexperience with this channel.

Most of us scurry away from disorientation. It's uncomfortable, confusing, and unsettling. The world as we know it has shifted from a house with solid floors, walls, and ceilings into a funhouse of distorting mirrors, undulating floors, a dearth of fun to those of us with a preference for stability and predictability. Yet there's great value to abiding in disorientation, doing so with patience and awareness because it's here that new understanding, growth, and creativity emerges.

Yet another model warrants mention due to its distinctive categories. Curious about what connects life across the planet, philosopher Guy Murchie recognizes not five but thirty-two senses which he divides into five unusual categories: radiation, feeling, chemical, mental, and spiritual. The categories, and my cursory attempt to explain them, contain unfamiliar combinations of abilities: radiation (includes seeing and sensing temperature and electromagnetic waves), feeling (includes hearing, proprioception, underwater sensing, and feeling the earth's rotation), chemical (smell, taste, appetite, sensing humidity), mental (language, navigation, time awareness, ability to play, navigation sense, and horticultural sense among many others), and spiritual (love, ecstasy, sin, sorrow, sacrifice and cosmic consciousness).

What is notable in these models is not so much their similarities as their differences, reinforcing the notion that there is no standard map for perceiving and that we are diverse in what we experience. The variations suggest that our blind-spots are much larger than a mere negligible smattering of spots and imply that vast regions with potentially great consequences are missing from our perceptual horizon. *(Exercises 2:2 Intelligences Evaluation)*

Notably the dominant sense for most of us is the eyes. Seeing, we say, is believing. The saying shows to what extent we rely on our eyes for evidence of phenomena. The cornea, cones, and optic nerves render the eyes a wondrous portal to the visible world. It is a marvelous function of the eyes to help us maneuver the strangle of a crowd at a concert and to reveal autumn's glorious blaze of burnt orange, red, and gold. But a sensory path that dominates perception also marginalizes underutilized paths. We overlook and possibly refute other paths of awareness. Note the oddity in the following statements: Touching is believing. Hearing is believing.

2. The Perceiving Body

Consider the discomfort associated with even a temporary lack of sight. Close your eyes and walk across the room. To compensate for the lack of seeing, our ears perk up for the slightest indication of sound. Our usual ability to balance may be compromised. We likely reach out with our arms, our skin sensors stretching into the unseen. How long does it take before unease compels you to reopen your eyes?

Deep Listening and Inner Senses

Deep somatic listening increases perceptual awareness on a multiplicity of sensory levels, opening our mind and body to phenomena previously ignored. The term implies using the ears, but is intended as a more complete sensory experience. We listen with our ears, but also our eyes, heart, gut, mind, and any other organ. We listen for recognizable phenomena and instances that defy words and ready understanding. We listen for nuance and subtlety. We listen deeply with the entirety of our being, no path ruled out, no clue or inkling of phenomena ignored. We root in the present moment and pay attention to any somatic event taking place now that captures attention or usually evades notice. We poke, prod and play, unwilling to accept easy conclusions that may—or likely does—exclude valuable information in the hinterlands of our attention. We notice thoughts, sensation and emotion. We notice breath and motion, proprioception and exteroception. We notice judgements, too, for instance, thinking we're too clumsy or dull, that imply bias. As impartially as possible, we witness the many events of our body.

A significant perceptual organ, one whose importance is not fully realized because of disembodied and limited understanding, is the skin. The skin is the largest organ of the body. The skin of an average adult weighs about eight pounds and would cover an area of about twenty-two square feet if stretched out on the floor. The skin is typically considered the physical boundary between who we are and who we are not.

We guard this boundary, societal and personal guidelines determining who we let near. There is a minimum of an eighteen inch safe zone between us and a stranger, a distance that is typical in many western countries. If that stranger were to come closer, the approach would be considered an infringement upon our personal space. We are selective about who shares this personal space with us. For good reason. Proximity sets off a chain reaction of physiological and psycho-emotional processes. A yellow light of caution, the red of halting, or the green of approval turns on. We need to quickly determine the stranger as friend or foe and if we should invite, flee, or fight. Our senses alerting us to the possible need to defend ourselves go on even higher alert with the event of touch, be the touch casual or prolonged and intimate. We need to determine the touch as safe and with the best of intentions. We are selective about who receives the key to our castle.

Among its functions, the skin helps to maintain our form and contains an extensive network of nerve cells. The skin helps to regulate our temperature, provide constant information about sensation, and support movement with its elasticity. Specific dermal cells act as a firewall that protects us from destructive microorganisms that lead to illness. The skin is an intricately complex porous web of connective tissue made up of a liquid crystalline material. This complex web extends throughout our body to every organ, bone, to our trillions of cells. Essentially, when someone touches us in one area, that person by extension is touching our entire body. "To touch the surface," says massage therapist Deane Juhan, "is to stir the depths."[7]

Cell biologist James Oschman believes the interconnectivity of the connective tissue is vital to understanding the working and potential of the entire body, a potential that is woefully undeveloped. He explains that "[t]here is no perspective that is more important than the systemic properties of the connective tissue and the relation of the connective tissue to the other systems in the body."[8] He points to the matter of our piezoelectricity, the fact that our porous liquid crystalline material conducts electricity.

The quality and strength of our electricity, our bioelectricitiy, is not something most of us ever think about, let alone feel in action. Yet the entire body conducts and radiates a variety of currents which, depending upon our activity, health, thoughts, and emotions, permeates our body and extends inches or a few impressive feet out from the skin. Types of measurable bioelectricity include light, sound, heat, chemical, gravity, and elasticity. Machines that measure a few of these currents include an electroencephalogram (EEG) for the brain and an electrocardiogram (EKG) for the heart, technology lagging in creating equipment to measure all types of currents.

Psychologist Rollin McCraty recognizes that the heart generates the largest bioelectric field of the body, its networks more complex than that of the brain. Forty-thousand neurons are contained in the heart, the same number of neurons as the brain. This information has profound implications for those who consider the brain the central computer of our body. McCraty points to research that reveals that more than half of our responses are the result of powerful currents generated by the heart. The implication of this is that the brain as the central computer our body, a popular metaphor for describing its function, is an outmoded portrayal.

The heart and brain share executive function of the body. The brain needs the heart the way an exhale needs the inhale. The heart is concerned with feeling, flow, and being. The brain is concerned with logic, processing, analysis, and doing. Both are important. Both are vital in helping us maneuver the complexity of living. Yet we tend to celebrate the brain and demean the heart. The heart is the seat of emotions. Displaying emotion, many mistakenly believe, is an indication of weakness, over sensitivity, or being touchy-feely, terms meant as insults, qualities associated as feminine, a derogatory characterization in male-centric, misogynist cultures. The brain, on the other hand, is hailed for its logic, processing, and analysis, qualities associated as masculine. We'd rather dismiss emotions, a natural and healthy body response, and overlook valuable somatic information supplied by the heart in favor of logic and its brethren. A cultural blind spot tainted by sexism is on full display here.

In ignoring the heart, we fail to use the skills associated with our emotional intelligence, among them an ability to recognize and regulate emotions and be an empathetic team player who uses criticism productively. Says psychologist Daniel Goleman, "If your emotional abilities aren't in hand, if you don't have self-awareness, if you are not able to manage your distressing emotions, if you can't have empathy and have effective relationships, then no matter how smart you are, you are not going to get very far."[9]

An organization that recognizes the importance of the heart is HeartMath Institute. Interested in heart-brain communication and its relationship to managing stress, the organization developed methods to bring heart electricity into coherence with the currents of the brain for excelling at healing, creativity and decision making. HeartMath founder Doc Childre explains, "The head can notice what things need to change, but the heart provides the power and direction to actually bring about the changes."[10] Eastern cultures have long placed the source of thought at the heart and those brought up in the East point to the heart area when using their word for mind.

Another center of power and sensitivity often overlooked is our gut. More and more research is being devoted to the enteric nervous system's vital role its 100 million neurons play on digestion and mood. Researcher and enterologist Michael Gershon refers to it as "the brain in our gut" and emphasizes that gut feelings are an accurate way to access a situation. With more nerve cells in our bowel than in our spine, the gut manufactures more than 30 neurotransmitters and continually sends messages to the brain through the vagus nerve. He says, "The enteric nervous system is also a vast chemical warehouse within which is represented every one of the classes of neurotransmitter found in the brain…. The multiplicity of neurotransmitters in the bowel suggests that the language spoken by the cells of the enteric nervous system is rich and brain-like in its complexity."[11] There's more to our gut feelings than we credit them.

Movement, Space and Inner Sense

Here is what interests me: Movement as well as touch profoundly impact the bioelectric charge. The frequency and quality of movement and touch keeps the connective tissues hydrated and reinforces what we experience as flexibility, vitality, and ease. Activated nerves send a host of information about who we are. Movement touches us. Touch moves us. Activated nerves flood us with information about our external as well as internal environment. We sense what is outside us, but also what is within. Access our connective tissues and somatic and kinetic worlds open. Says fiction writer Haruki Murakami, "I move, therefore I am."[12]

For many of us, bioelectricity goes undetected without the assistance of a machine not because this electricity is imperceptible but because we have not tuned into it. We have yet to switch to the appropriate awareness channel or to develop our somatic intelligence. Once we do and move with awareness of our macro- and micro-movements, listening deeply enough, devoting attention to developing our somatic intelligence, we sense how the largest organ of our body communicates. We discover micro-movements always taking place. We discover the impact of motion. We discover patterns of movement that hint at a core organizing belief. We discover connections among sensation, motion, and emotion. We discover missing information previously in our blind spot now in the foreground that can put us in touch with a fundamental part of who we are. (*Exercise 2:3 Detecting Energy*)

Within reach of our hands, the entire area reachable by our limbs, is our kinesphere, a term coined by Rudolph Laban, dancer, movement theorist, and founder of Labanotation, a notation system for recording and analyzing human movement that includes terminology aimed at expanding a dancer's spatial orientation. The kinesphere, the area outside the body, also referred to as negative space by visual artists, gets us to notice how we use and engage with it. In contrast, the body is considered positive space. The relationship between the two gets us to notice how our movement not only determines the shape of our body but also shapes the space around us. (*Exercise 2:4 Positive and Negative Space*)

The negative space around our body is not empty as Oschman and others point out, but full of all types of bioelectricity. This area, referred to as our biofield, a term coined by the National Institute of Health to describe the interplay of electromagnetic patterns and consciousness, is not densely physical like our body, but is full of radiating currents. The biofield permeates every part of our physical body and emits its current, which commingle biofields outside us.

Those of us whose awareness channels are sensitively attuned to the biofield perceive not only when someone has entered this space but can also perceive its contents. It can be viewed with the eyes, felt with the hands, and sensed with inner senses. No wonder entering into someone's biofield is such a touchy subject. Unknowingly we may be stepping on bioelectric toes.

Advances in understanding have occurred since Perception 101. There is a type of seeing that doesn't rely on eyes, hearing that doesn't rely on ears, touch that does not require skin upon skin, a knowing that arrives from the gut. We all experience this to a degree. Most of us can point to a time, for instance, when we picked up on a "vibe" coming from a stranger who walked into the room which led to a conclusion about their character that was not based on a conversation or any of the usual ways of knowing. We use vague language like "vibe" or "hunch" to validate without needing to explain our claim. Our hunches may prove accurate, and Gershon among others would encourage following our body's signals, yet we tend to discount them as irrelevant. We belittle this type of perception. We do so because it likely falls into one of the undeveloped intelligences. "There are things known and there are things unknown, and in between are the doors of perception," says poet William Blake.[13] My suspicion is that we are using our senses, but the processing speed, from incoming stimuli to bringing it to consciousness, is lightning fast, the velocity of the neural circuitry not easily trackable. We are deceived as we can be with film, which is a series of still frames giving the viewer the illusion of continuous motion, our eye unable to see individual frames unless the projector slows down.

The olfactory sense, our ability to smell, is the fastest of our senses and the most direct. The olfactory response is immediate whereas other senses traveling via neurons along the spinal cord are comparatively slow in reaching the brain. Smell is connected to the limbic system which deals with instinctive or automatic behaviors. Education theorist Gloria Rodriguez-Gil believes that smell has very little impact on conscious thought. I'm not so sure. I suspect there are innumerable impressions, hunches and potentials for knowing that remain in our blind spot discounted because we have not been trained to attend to them.

What mechanisms operate beyond superficial impressions? Which of our conclusions are the result of reliance upon a dominant intelligence that overshadows the utility of others? The smallest of bodily events, a plucked tendon, a swelling, a twinge, the fleeting, initially inexplicable surfacing of a thought, emotion, or image may—or may not—catch our attention. At what point do atoms and cells become detectable? When does nothing become something? The strength of the inner organs of perception is slowly catching up to the physical organs of perception. This inner organs of perception includes the inner eyes, inner ears, fascia, and connective tissue, and senses not associated in the usual way with a specific organ. This type of sensing is underutilized, therefore skills associated with them are weak. It's understandable that many would conclude that such perceptions don't exist.

We may readily discount what is not understood until an experience pushes its evidence further. For example, while in attendance at a dance retreat, my body energized and sensitive from hours and days of exertion, I watched wide-eyed as glass-like shards broke off from a fellow dancer's body and fell to the floor. I was well aware that my physical eyes were not doing the seeing, but what was operating riddled me. I might have discounted the incident as imagined or the result of a fatigued body, but when she later explained her dance as clearing illusions from the body, my curiosity piqued. I recognized that my inner senses were perceiving what my eyes did not. My usual reliance on my verbal intelligence which occludes other ways of perceiving gave way in that moment. I've since learned to welcome this sense which has strengthened with time and practice and apply it to energy healing with clients and being able to "see" their life or feel their emotions or sensations without them verbally sharing the information.

The body continually communicates; it's up to us to pay attention. We all can develop this ability. Inner sensing is a type of deep listening that perceives the subtle, less obvious cues. Deep somatic listening transforms a fleeting awareness into an insight, weak ability into a strong ability, an unnoticed perception into an open pathway. Deep listening grounds ourselves in the five senses and extends to picking up on the nuances, noticing the perceptions that dwell in the hinterlands of our attention, those that are likely poorly understood by more conventional perceptual models. Once we develop such attention, once we recognize our habits and open ourselves to other pathways. Our somatic intelligence increases and ushers in a new view, a new touch, new moves, and a renewed us.

Somatic Attuning

The body is continually sharing its knowledge. It sends and receives innumerable signals on every level of being. It is up to each of us to open our sensory pathways, to notice and interpret the body's signals, both what our body emits as well as what it picks up from beyond the skin. Consciously detecting and understanding the body's signals is somatic literacy. Reading the signals helps us decipher conditions of our body and determine beneficial actions for optimizing health and leading a satisfying life. For most of us however, our somatic literacy is negligible, allowing us to get by with fulfilling a modicum of daily needs such as eating, drinking and sleeping, although even these are prone to static as evidenced by the many who suffer from eating and sleep disorders. If we turn away from body signals, somatic illiteracy impoverishes the body and mind, and our potential is cut short.

The wealth of information and knowing at our fingertips, in our heart, in our gut, in our movement, is available when we turn our attention, when we train ourselves to deeply listen. Opening to these pathways supports thriving. Opening the senses to the vast array of information expands and refines what we know.

It is necessary that we pay heed to the full array of our senses but to attend first to our primary senses. Establish this foundation as requisite to ensure that circumstances don't easily throw us off and that if we lose balance it is readily regained. A solid foundation handles growth and stress and the inevitability of changes. A solid foundation sustains our body in readiness and resiliency. Sensitivity to our primary senses is grounding, embodying, a living with our mind, dwelling in the entirety of our body and feeling the wellspring of our personal being.

For these reasons, it is beneficial to practice somatic attuning. Somatic attuning is a practice of bringing our internal world in sync with the external world. We establish a way to cultivate and sustain harmony and sympathetic resonance. We adjust to continuously changing circumstances to experience balance and flow.

Somatic attuning is not something that gets accomplished once and is done. Like eating which we do daily for sustenance, somatic attuning is an ongoing practice of checking in with our body and performing a felt sensory inventory. We notice what is going on and make adjustments as necessary. It means reading the body signals and providing ourselves with the movement or sleep or postural change deemed helpful. A felt sensory inventory can be done while still or moving, while driving to work or stretching in the dance studio. Ultimately the practice becomes so common that we have access with a moment's notice.

One of the most important indicators of well-being and the difference between minimal and maximal function is our breath. If we overlook all else and attune only to breath, we are already at an advantage. Breath acts as an adhesive for mind, body, and energy. Shift the breath and the body and energy follows. We typically take 12 to 20 breaths per minute. Short, shallow breath is often an indication of disturbances such as anxiety, stress, and asthma. Deep, smooth breath brings about ease and allows the body time enough to recharge. *(Exercise 2.4: Breath Counts)*

The patterns of our breath are a telltale sign of the condition of our body. Restriction and shallowness are common responses to fear. A startle response stops the breath temporarily, but if the hold is prolonged and becomes a pattern, as often happens with trauma, we cut ourselves off from vital sustenance. Noticing and shifting our breath is among the easiest ways to bring more energy into our body and strengthen the life force. It can be the difference between surviving and thriving, between lethargy and invigoration. A dramatic example of this is Hal, a baseball player, who shared with me late in the semester that he recognized his breath pattern was consistently shallow. As a high school freshman, he developed pectus excavatum, a collapsing of the chest wall. A fellow classmate made fun of him in the locker room and as a result, he vowed to not remove his shirt in front of anyone again. If pectus excavatum is left untreated, the chest wall can squeeze the lungs and heart with fatal consequences. Sure enough, over the next several years, his breast bone turned more inward, pressing against his organs, yet he kept his condition a secret from his parents, doctor, and baseball coach. Exercises in class got him to acknowledge the shallowness of breath and the shame of his emotional and physical pain. He realized, too, the potentially fatal repercussions of continuing to ignore his body. He subsequently spoke to his parents and doctors and arranged for surgery, aware that this class may have saved his life.

Turning his attention to his body didn't require extraordinary skill. It required that he be present to the sensations, actions, and emotions of his body, to notice and face his shame and use that information to make the smart decision of getting medical help. It required that he attune somatically to the specific conditions of his body and feel the truths however uncomfortable manifesting in the moment.

Rising Above Deceit into Truth

It is easy to deceive ourselves, give undue weight to the perceptual noise, and sideline the truths of the body. Perceptual noise includes old, unresolved emotional and physical pain that eclipses connecting to the stimuli of the present moment. It includes compromising healthy lasting balance for a false and temporary gain. It may include yielding to fear, anger, weakness, blame, and shame without following up with a path toward recuperating balance. It may include inflating our importance above others or belittling our own needs. It may include a rigid, unmoving body and mind. It may include operating under the guise of denying the existence of blind spots or pushing beyond healthy limits. It may include closing our eyes to the repercussions of our actions and failing to recognize our role in a group, family, or any other collection of living beings. It may include clenching and contracting the body as if pinched by laundry clips and refusing to acknowledge their discomfort. It may include slumping and not giving breath an open passage.

Somatic attuning helps us define perceptual noise, heal unresolved wounds, and discern the difference between a fleeting bodily response and a detrimental belief system or defense pattern that has outlived its usefulness. The original pattern, for instance, slouching while sitting, which likely helped us adapt to circumstances years earlier, now gets in the way. Most of us operate from a schema, an underlying organization pattern that manifests through our thoughts, actions, and motion. Recognizing the pattern and opening to new input and expression frees us from its usually unconscious hold upon our body and allows us to respond anew each moment.

Somatic attuning helps us recognize which actions unfold awareness that align with our best interests. Somatic attuning asks that we be forthright and impartial. We connect with the felt body experience. We inquire. We welcome the feelings, sensations, and perceptions impartially. Just see, notice, feel, move. We attend to ourselves with curiosity. We engage with actions that bring shadow into the light and turn the light brilliant.

The body does not lie. It welcomes and awaits our attention. Unrestrained at birth, the body wants to continue its turns of phrase and motion, to walk and gesture and express and be its best, its every hope and dream, its strength and vulnerability, the complexity of cells and bones and breath functioning without impediment.

Its desire to lie on a soft bed for sleep or rise from a chair and sprint across a field welcomes our attention. Its desire to rest or run, to provoke or play, essentially to admit its truths welcomes our attention. Something as simple as sitting beneath a tree or walking barefooted on the beach can be profound when we somatically attune. Stillness moves and quiets us. Moving stills and enlivens us. Our body shows the way. Its signs are everywhere.

The Balance of Grounding and Centering

The practice of balance has widespread beneficial ramifications. Of utmost importance, balance assists in the avoidance of injury. It increases range of motion, strength, and coordination, reduces tension and fatigue, and allows us to respond to difficulty with flexibility. Physicist and founder of Feldenkrais Method, a body mechanics system, Moshe Feldenkrais says, "A body in a state of equilibrium is alive and dynamic, even in repose, continually moving in reaction to the forces on and inside of it, playing between the balance and counterbalance."[14]

With somatic attuning, we practice awareness of these forces, learning when to yield and when to resist, when to bend and when to stand tall. Our body is undergoing constant change but so too is everything around us, people, objects, settings, situations, temperature, an endless array of predictable and unpredictable circumstances requiring that we root attention in the present moment with a firm but pliant body. Firmness and pliancy may sound contradictory but it's exactly these opposing forces that allow for adaptation to the inevitability of change. To reinforce pliant stability, there are two commonly recommended foundational practices, grounding and centering.

Grounding is a practice of balance and integration free of undue stress that emphasizes a solid, mutually supported relationship with the earth. Grounding, as the term implies, emphasizes a direct relationship with the earth. We experience gravity holding us in place, our weight pressing downward through our bones, posture, and musculature. The axis of our spine roots downward but also extends upward, the architecture of our body situated between earth and sky.

When grounded, we cannot be knocked over, or not readily. If balance is lost, there is also immediate recovery. Grounding is visible in a gymnast who, after hurling herself into the air for tumbling, a highly disorienting move, lands squarely on her feet. It is visible in dancers as they navigate space and the press of other bodies. It is at work when we climb or descend stairs, when we push our chair, when we extend a handshake with another, and when we are still.

Grounding helps the body function optimally, our spine with minimal or no compression, each vertebra from tail bone to the top of our neck soft and extended, no part of the body impeding nerve communication nor blocking energy flow. Body systems function optimally. Grounding helps us to feel at ease, the support of the earth working in our behalf. Research on grounding is shown to have many physiological benefits, among them deeper, more restful sleep, and reduced inflammation. Those at the Earthing Institute use the word "earthing" instead of "grounding" and promote being barefoot with the ground (or wearing shoes made from natural fabrics) as a way to generate an exchange of electrons. They site innumerable benefits, among them strengthening the immune system and recharging our bioelectric currents.

Grounding involves sending imagined roots from our feet into the earth. We stand (or sit) firmly upright to help distribute our weight evenly and support the many bones of the body. While standing we engage the plantar fascia, the metatarsal bones of each toe, broaden the heels, and allow a tiny lift. We feel the spread of the sole of the foot upon the surface of the floor. Within seconds, its repercussion as a dynamic, energizing position becomes apparent. *(Exercise 2.4: Grounding)*

Centering is similar to grounding in that it also supports balance, however with an emphasis on physiological and emotional equilibrium. The practice of centering reinforces psycho-emotional resiliency, poise, and integration and establishes an inner space of resilient calm. A person who is centered rolls with life's joys and upsets. Consider the challenge of public speaking as an example, an activity so frightful for many that we'd rather hide in our room than break out in shivers and sweat or worse at the podium. When centered, we acknowledge any fears and apply the tools we know that help, such as slowing breath and grounding. *(Exercise 2.5: Centering)*

Grounding and centering are like the sea grass at the ocean bottom that sways with the tides. When grounded and centered, we adapt to the tides as well as the trips and punches, the leaps and laughs. We adapt to what comes our way while maintaining integrity. Every moment becomes an opportunity to listen deeply, to connect with our body, to feel and see and touch what matters.

Our body will do what it needs to do to get our attention. It will knock and holler, and up the ante as necessary to get us to approach the door and open to embodying ourselves. Best if we attend to the knock before any escalation of signals. Best if we learn how to heed the call. Best if we learn how to minimize the expenditure of our energy and maximize our potential.

When we tune in to our body, we uncover an amazing resource. We learn to balance objective knowing with subjective knowing. We find in our body the grain of sand that leads to the universe. We find paths that lead to knowing, embodiment, healing, and creativity.

If we take the step. If we attend to the path. If we listen.

Some of us tune in because we are drawn by curiosity and a desire to express ourselves creatively. Others go for health reasons. You must find your own reason. Your life, your body, and your embodiment await you.

Exercises

2:1 Primary Senses Sitting Awareness

- Find a place where you can sit without engaging in activity or chatting with anyone. The space could public or private place, in doors or outside. Set a timer for 10 minutes.
- Hear: Put attention on your ears. Feel the vibration of sound. Follow the vibrations as they resonate or ripple through your body. Identify the source such as blue jay or truck, and name the sound such as squawk or rumble. What is the difference between hearing and naming?
- See: Put attention on your eyes. Feel the effect of light on your cornea. Let your eyes dart around, then let them linger on one spot. What is the difference between darting and lingering?
- Touch: Put attention on your hands. Graze nearby surfaces and investigate texture, temperature, and any other characteristics. What feelings at your wrist, arm, or elsewhere emanates from your hands? How do your clothes feel against your skin?
- Smell: Put attention on your nose. What is the sensation of air passing in and out of your nostrils? What scents are detectable? What does your skin smell like, the wall, this book? As you inhale, track the influence of scents upon your body.
- Taste: Put attention on your mouth. What does your saliva taste like? Can you detect any flavors left over from a previous meal?
- Emotion: Put attention on your heart. What emotions do you detect? Where other than your heart do you feel them?
- Thought: Put attention on your thoughts. What is passing through your mind? What ones hang around? Where in your body do they resonate?
- Let your attention roam wherever it wishes to go. Witness without interference or direction.
- *Variation:* Follow the same sequence as above but write impressions.

2:2 Intelligences Evaluation

- Make a list of common intelligences and ones you believe should be included.
- With each intelligence, give yourself a S for Strong, A for Average, and U for Undeveloped.
- Review your assessment. What does it say about how you perceive and navigate the world? How do you imagine your perceptions and beliefs might change if you devoted time to strengthening the weaker intelligences?

2:3 Detecting Energy

- Rub your hands together for several seconds as if warming them after a cold outing.
- Separate your hands a few inches apart, one facing the other. Repeatedly move your hands closer, then apart until you feel energy. The energy is commonly felt as tingles or a magnetic pull. What other sensations do you notice?

2:4 Positive and Negative Space Movement

- You may want music to accompany this exercise. Move your body using minimal effort. Sway, rock, step, undulate, or do any other movement that arises in the moment.
- Visualize the shape your body is making. You may use a mirror.
- Continue moving but turn awareness to the space immediately round you and visualize how your movements shape the space. You may use a mirror.
- Write about what you noticed when you moved with awareness of positive versus negative space.

2:5 Breath Counts

- Set a timer for a minute. Count each time you inhale. Because results will vary with your attention, repeat the count a few times to get an average.
- Most of us breathe too fast. See what happens when you deliberately slow your breath. With each inhale, invite breath into your diaphragm and belly. Deliberately prolong your inhales.
- Extend your exhalations. Contract your diaphragm slightly to expel more air. If you get dizzy, return to normal breathing. Repeat these extended breaths for several minutes.
- What feels different in your back, belly, lungs, head or anywhere else? What influence does it have on your emotions and sense of calm?
- Speed up your inhalations and exhalations. Do this briefly, no longer than a minute. What do you notice?

2:6 Grounding

- Stand. Place your feet solidly upon the floor. Wiggle your toes. Rock from toes to heals to settle into place and distribute your weight. Engage the plantar fascia, the metatarsal bones, broaden the heels, and allow a tiny lift.
- Bend your knees slightly.
- Tilt your pelvis side to side, then front to back before returning to stillness.

- Put awareness on your tail bone and make your way up, vertebra by vertebra. Lift upward, imagining space and water entering the area around each disk.
- Expand your chest. Take in a few rounds of breath. Let your arms hang easily from your clavicle.
- Extend the vertebra at your neck. Float your head upon the last vertebra.
- Feel both an upward and downward pull. Notice any areas of tension. Invite breath to reach those sites.
- Relax lips, jaw, gaze and brow.
- Stay in the position for a few minutes, making any necessary adjustments to maintain an effortless but strong position.
- Imagine opening the soles of your feet to the energy of the earth. Send roots down from the soles of your feet through the floor into the ground.
- *Variation:* Do the same outside with bare feet.

2:7 Centering Exercise

- You can do this exercise laying on your back, sitting, or standing. Relax into the chosen position, giving permission to any tension in your body to release.
- Invite breath to your heart and take several easy breaths.
- Take several easy breaths with attention at your solar plexus.
- Take several easy breaths at the area just below your belly.
- Adjust your position as needed for comfort.
- Choose a word that epitomizes calm. You can also choose an image instead or a color that is appealing. With each inhale, invoke this word.
- Choose a word that epitomizes a pattern of behavior that no longer serves you. You can also choose an image or color instead. With every exhale, invoke this word
- After several rounds of breath, return to normal breathing. Notice any sensations, images, words, memories, or feelings that arise.
- Write about any part of the experience. Write about what you found that delights or confuses you.

3

The Kinesthetic Body

I want to share what took place before I sat down to write this chapter: I moved. On the carpet near the chair, my feet grounded, my spine lengthened, I inhaled deeply and listened to the desires of my body, impulses that spurred action. I followed through. My body arched the back gently, a slow stretch which resulted in two small relieving pops from my thoracic vertebrae. My arms then lifted parallel to my ears, palms facing each other, then facing out to initiate the arms' slow descent, my chest expanding. The motion felt strengthening and opening, calming and energizing. I repeated the motion, savoring each breath, blood rushing from hands when overhead, back in when lowered. I paused at shoulder height to extend my hands further with emphasis on the middle fingers which elongated my arms, engaged my biceps, and energized me. I let my body determine what followed, quick darting motions, small undulations, neck tilting down, then up. I surrendered to flow and the natural rhythms of my body. With motion undirected, I settled into a balance of guiding with watching and allowing and eventually returned to simple standing. My body called for this sequence of movements. I listened. I let it have its way. The connectivity propelled me forward. Satisfied, refreshed, and eager to get writing, I turned on my computer.

Moving is a way I access my writing and my mind. It's also my way out of the clutter of thinking into clarity. I connect. From the sometimes too airy disconnect of thought, I settle into my flesh. I feel my body in motion. I use moving to get to my words; that was today's intention. Another time, I may get up from my chair for the singular purpose of moving and feeling who I am. I have danced in most rooms of my house, in the backyard, on sidewalks and city streets, dance studios and stages. An audience of one, myself, is sufficient. I do not need the gaze of another. I need to feel the intimacy of myself in the unfolding of becoming.

We are always moving. As you read these words, your eyes dart from one side of the page to the other. Your lungs and torso contract and expand with each breath. You may have pursed your lips or shifted in your seat. You may quiver, hiccup, flinch, cross your legs and traverse the room. Perhaps you feel the pump of blood through your veins. These are copious bodily events detectable once you tune your attention inward.

On a more subtle level, beyond casual detection, is additional motion. Neurons are firing, hormones and enzymes secreting, heart, brain, and other organs radiating energy. Blood, breath, cells, and atoms flow, respire, and vibrate. At any given moment, a complexity of autonomic events is taking place to maintain the body while primary attention is focused on a more obvious activity like reading. Absolute stillness does not exist. Even while sitting, sleeping, or standing still, we are moving.

There is a distinctive experience that arises from somatic attuning. When we tie attention to our moving body, to visible and subtle motions, we expand understanding of the self and everything that comprises who we are. Consciousness brightens with sparks from the unconscious. We access a treasure trove of hidden influences and motivation. We tap into the core of our being, the force of our own currents, the life pulse, a force simultaneously connected to all that exists within and beyond the perimeter of our skin.

This tapping into the life pulse is a subjective experience. It is a type of introspection, an idea that may prompt squirms, given our cultural bias toward extroversion. A more complete understanding and appreciation of the quiet gifts of introversion, much of it in our blind spot, has begun. Bigger and louder are often considered better, the life of the party commanding attention and accolades. Bigger and louder more readily captures the attention of others. Attention to the quiet of introversion, to the subjective phenomenon of our body, requires a deliberate focus that turns away from the loud and obvious. We go to another room and close the door. We step outside under the shade of a tree.

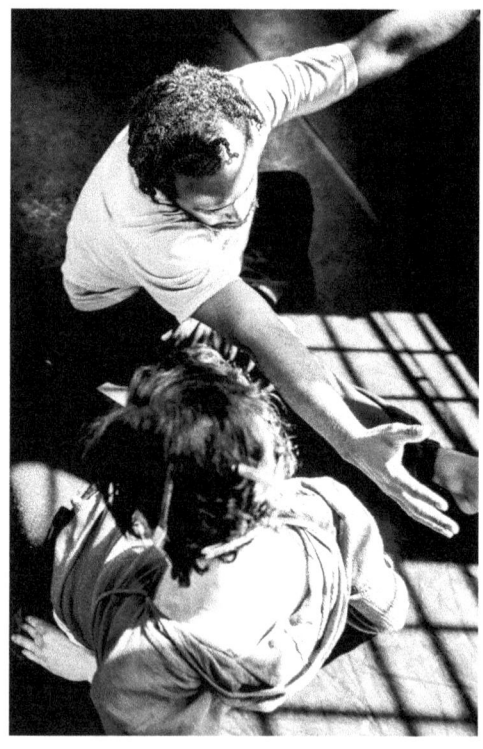

Aaron Brown, top, Fieval Nihm

3. The Kinesthetic Body

We lower our eye lids to close off our usual focus. We listen deeply to the heart beat, blood flow, and the rise and fall of sensation. We listen deeply to ourselves to hear the body's requests.

This deliberate shift can have monumental repercussions. In turning attention toward subtle stimuli while grounding and centering, we align inwardly to the inner world. The fine threads inherent to the weave of our humanity, creativity and health begin to appear. Time spent investigating the folds and currents of our flesh opens us to the subjective somatic world, to our life pulse, and to the larger world. In coming to better know ourselves, we can see—and hear and feel—beyond our skin with greater clarity, the universal accessible through the particulars of our body, the universe trembling in the palm of our hand.

It's not an either/or, subjective or objective, but a conjunction on a grand scale. We operate with both perspectives. We are both an individual with our own name, address, and social security number and an inextricable part of a family, community, nation, and ecosystem. We are a star in a constellation, a light in a diamond latticework, a collection of atoms among an infinitely larger collection, a voice in a community, a body developing and decaying in the cycle of life, our personal rhythm in and out of synch with other rhythms.

An approach to moving is to continually be in warm up mode. We are always just beginning. We are always stretching and flexing, testing range of motion, exploring position and balance, strength and weakness, curious when phenomena arises. Regardless of experience and circumstance, we are always starting afresh. Notice, for instance, resistance and boredom. Notice pain and shortness of breath. Notice temperature change. Notice a shift in attention, emotion, and sensation. Keep going, one movement after another, an eye on the life pulse until movement takes on a momentum of its own. *(Exercise 3.1: Simple Warmup)*

Choreographer Deborah Hay finds motion liberating, especially when done without preconceptions or the need to control. It's a matter of focusing on the desires of the body to move and letting go of thoughts. Only move. Only body. She says, "The weight of my bones, organs, muscles, and joints endlessly spread onto the floor. There are 206 bones in the human body, 26 in each foot. Joints break open. Tongue dissolves. Throat disappears. I abandon holding onto the shape of me. I am movement without looking for it."[1]

To feel most alive, dancer and choreographer Martha Graham says, "In order to work, in order to be excited, in order to simply be, you have to reborn to the instant. You have to permit yourself to feel, you have to permit yourself to feel vulnerable. You may not like what you see, that is not important …

you must know how to animate the body."[2] A way to feel that enlivening is to connect to the life pulse.

The Life Pulse

The life pulse is a subtle and sometimes bold energy that continually flows throughout the body. It's what gives us that sense of vitality when its flow runs strong and lethargy when the flow is blocked. The strength of our life pulse determines if we feel purposeful or lost, in touch with our body and surroundings or out of touch. Moving with somatic awareness is a way to ensure our current remains strong, fluid, and steady.

Anyone who has been bed bound or suffered a broken limb knows the liberating joy that comes with regaining mobility. But even without a physical challenge, the sensations that accompany moving can be uplifting. Movement taking place for its own sake allows the body its natural inclinations. Movement that takes into account sensations and emotions is what gives us power to connect to choice and recognize our body as a great resource. This approach to movement reveals the body as a conduit of freedom of expression, balance, and adaptability. We work with ourselves, not against. We enter the flow of being and knowing, feeling and becoming.

Oblivious to her own sensory phenomena, my student Lisa is similar to many other students during their first few days of class. She responded with astonishment when a fellow student noted feeling a slight pain in her eye while dancing. "How can you feel that," Lisa asked while looking for visible evidence in the eyes. "I don't even feel a headache coming until it's full blown." Several class sessions later, Lisa, too, discovered a depth of sensation in her body which opened the way to bending more easily and releasing a previously ignored constriction in her back.

Our sensations are communicating to us continually. It's up to us to listen and use their offerings. It's up to us to notice and engage with them.

Children move readily with ease. Impulsively they leap into a puddle, slide down stairs, rock while sitting. There is pliancy to their movement that is not separate from who they are. Their movements arise naturally and spontaneously. It's how they learn about their body and their surroundings. Often linked to playing, their movements are fully engrossing and rely on the entirety of their being, no motion or part of themselves excluded.

Any parent knows how difficult it is to still a child in motion. For us, the challenge may be the opposite. Lost en route to adulthood, after parents and teachers reprimanded us to sit or stand still is the movement connection to the life pulse and to all the wisdom that comes with a felt connection to our flesh. For many of us, expressive movement may have vanished to the point that an invitation to dance at a party provokes anxiety. "Can't" or "won't" is the response I often get from friends to whom I extend an invitation, a reason I continually use the word "movement" rather than "dance," the former less intimidating than the latter. Lost is the life affirming connection, a natural expression of being, an organismic joy of motion. Our once innate ability to move gets sullied and replaced by a lulling stillness which stiffens us with age.

The more in touch we are with the many layers of our body, the more in touch we are with our balance, our voice, our motion, our gifts, and the awe of being alive. It can be a source of wisdom, a wellspring of creativity and healing. Movement is a powerful way we learn about ourselves. Movement is how we engage the universe of our body.

Doing and Being

To tap into the body's wisdom and learn how our body communicates, it is helpful to alternate between two modes, doing and being. Both are necessary and beneficial.

Doing involves asserting, guiding, intending, shaping, and controlling. Its attention is singularly focused. When we create an agenda or fix points along a journey, we are doing. When we control or guide a situation, we are doing. Doing likes to analyze situations and determine strategies. Doing is interested in results, long-term vision, and repercussions for the future.

Being involves allowing, yielding, watching, sensing, and flowing. Its attention is open. Being is reflected in how we show up for an agenda or journey, the particulars revealed with time. Being is concerned about the moment— this moment. It prefers to surrender to whim and momentum. Being has no agenda other than to be present and to change course as wanted or needed.

Being and doing are complementary much like east and west, right and left, sun and moon. One enhances and needs the other. Western culture applauds doing and getting things done. We often ask, "What are you doing?" "What have you done?" Or "What do you do?" Answers to these questions come readily. How we respond, typically with a list of activities, achievements, and works in progress puts us in a favorable or unfavorable light by the questioner. We often get criticized for not doing enough. Overdoing it, working long hours, burning the proverbial candle at both ends, is frequently considered impressive despite how it disrupts and compromises well-being.

Being receives less attention and less support. When was the last time you were asked, "How is your being?" Or "What are you being?" So culturally unfamiliar, there's no idiomatic phrases for such questions, my own attempts admittedly awkward. Figuring out how to answer them may provoke a lengthy response—which I would welcome—or a raised eyebrow and a polite withdrawal from the conversation.

We spend an inordinate amount of time and effort in doing and treat being like a neglected, undeserving stepchild. The closest most of us get to being is during vacation. Even then however, we don't give it its due. The vacation is too short or packed with scheduled activities, and by the time we're relaxed enough to open to being, it's time to refill our suitcase and return home.

Doing is comforting and familiar and comes with expectations and objectives. Being is unsettling because there are few or no expectations. Being is what is already happening and changing moment to moment. We may laugh or we may leap. We may take a nap or run on the beach. We may use our attention to track the sharpness in the eye as it migrates to a tension in the neck and a clenched jaw. Even those of us who may complain about everything we must do, walk the dog, clean the house, go to work, pay bills, change the computer passwords yet again, may experience anxiety when we finally take time out for the unfamiliarity of being. Ironically, we end up not knowing what to do, the connection to being tenuous, getting into its flow initially riddled by aborted starts, doubt, and unease. "Am I *doing* it right," ask many of my students when I suggest an activity that focuses on being.

With being, there is no right and no wrong. There is only What Is. This moment yawning, the next moment leaning on the left leg, followed by a sigh, then a momentary worry, then guilt about not returning a phone call, then lifting the pen to write a few paragraphs, and so forth. Being is a stream of moments which welcomes inclusion of the unconscious whereas doing aims for willful, conscious actions.

Great benefit can come from movements we initiate, from voluntary, deliberate acts of doing. Great benefit can also come from witnessing activity already taking place, from acts of being. I'm not referring to the difference between parasympathetic and autonomic activity, but to the difference between setting a series of actions into motion like deciding to walk to the car or deciding to raise an arm, versus witnessing what is already underway, like how I leaned closer to the computer while typing the last phrase and then rested my chin in my hand. Choosing movements as well as recognizing those already taking place cultivates awareness of the movement channel and develops our somatic intelligence.

Doing and being are both required for developing somatic literacy. Doing supplies the focus and container while being provides the content. Doing suggests determining ahead of time the application of a given focus. Being is what shows up. Together they contribute to a unifying whole, two poles dancing around each other, each offering their complementary gifts, the give and the take, the expected and the unforeseen, the known and the unknown, all emerging in the moment. They tap into the full body, all body systems in use, cells humming along, no synaptic route overused. Together they ensure the laying of new synaptic routes, increased brain plasticity and increased pliancy with every limb and step. They ensure that the rhythms of the body renew and adapt, inspire and respire, rest and stir awake. *(3:2 Doing and Being Exercise)*

Focused and Open Attention

Similar to doing and being are focused attention and open attention. Focused attention is what the term implies. There is an object, a focus for our deep listening, a region of the body that receives our attention. Our attention turns, for example, to our ankle to sense what is happening at the joint. We investigate. We control to a degree what takes place. We may sense its shape and look for sensation. We may rotate the ankle and point our toes to see how motion effects what is detected. We repeat the motion to notice subtle distinctions, perhaps wiggling the big toe or flexing them all.

Open attention is broad. There is no specific object of focus and much less control. Rather, we survey the horizon of awareness to see what appears. Attention may be drawn to the ankle, then the toe, then to hearing the hum in the room, then remembering a line from a favorite song, then noticing

Opening attention: Amy Impellizzeri

heat at our neck. We track attention as it wanders inward and outward. There is no goal, lofty, simple, or otherwise. No judgements or expectations either. We engage in being and do little more than witness.

Both types of attention raise awareness and lead to knowing how and what our body is communicating. Both provide vital information. Both contribute to increasing consciousness.

It is helpful to recognize the natural inclinations of open attention as well as notice any changes that take place once limits are applied for focused attention. Noting differences between them is trickier than it sounds. Any type of attention alters the object of our attention, a personal version of quantum theory's Schrodinger's Cat which shows a particle's behavior as indeterminate until its probability wave collapses upon observation. In other words, the act of observing affects what takes place. Even a prompt to be spontaneous tests our ability to be spontaneous. It's a challenge to pretend to not look while looking. As soon as you look, a focus is established and removed from elsewhere. But we're not seeking absolute or objective truth. We're looking to notice patterns in the puzzle of motion, sensation, and emotion. We're looking at motion.

There is always an experience already taking place awaiting detection by our senses. Breathing takes place without our decision to breath.

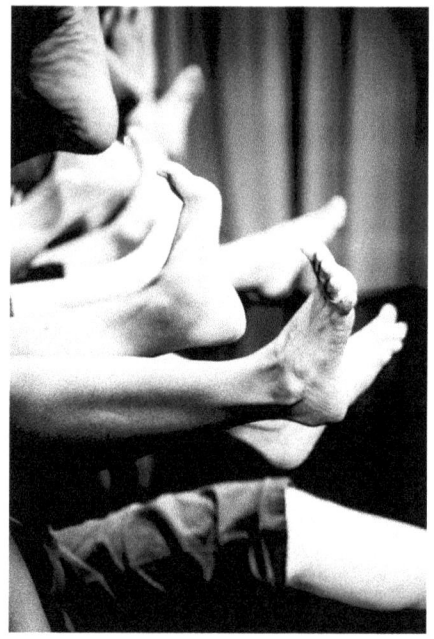

Feet chatter

Practicing stillness: Cheryl Pallant

Yet once we shift our attention to the particulars of our breath, it frequently changes, sometimes getting more labored until it returns to its original unobserved rhythm. Or notice how your eyes dart across the page, the space around you, as well as your inner space as you read. Were your eyes already darting in this way or did my instruction and your attention change how they move?

Performing a body scan helps to inventory what is taking place. A body scan, informative in what it reveals, is like taking an x-ray but without the expensive equipment. The scan registers our contents, our tensions, emotions, and other body phenomena, and promotes coming to know our somatic self. We may do it once; better yet to do it repeatedly and compare results. *(Exercise 3:3 Body Scan)*

We can learn much about ourselves from sensing what is already taking place, in aligning attention to the effortless now of presence. What is happening with our seeing, hearing, and such? The longer we devote to this practice, the greater our sensitivity, a strengthening of the muscle of attention. We go from noticing the obvious like the placement of our hand to noticing details like the shadows between our fingers, how an area of tissue in our shoulder for which there is no name relaxes, how an incremental expansion in our lungs spikes energy, how increasing flexibility in our hamstring or lengthening the spine prompts a restorative sigh. We become curious. We notice feelings that hadn't shown their face previously and access energy we didn't know existed. Habits and patterns are recognized along with the choice of their untangling. We may find associations in how we hold our body, move, or emote, in what we think and believe, a single glimpse functioning like a fractal providing access to the whole. We participate consciously in the stream of our being. We show up for ourselves. We learn about the matter of our body. We embody.

Experiences we deliberately create, on the other hand, become a sort of laboratory or playground in which we can identify factors that limit and shape experience. We come to these experiences with expectation, a question in pursuit of answer, a proposal to investigate, a structure or prompt, parameters and guidelines. Deep somatic listening is given a focus.

Both approaches encourage exploring obvious and subtle sensory events. Both approaches return us to the home of our body, to its truth and its deflections of the truth, to what we sense and attempt to draw meaning from, to what we know without doubt and what we hold as suspect. Creativity lies in all. Creativity lies in the tension between opposites, in the discomfort of not knowing, in feeling unfamiliarity and familiarity yet forging ahead anyway, in pushing forward and in letting go. Creativity thrives in asserting and allowing, extending an effort and seeing what shows up. Creativity relies on generating structures and identifying the linchpins to fortify the structure or collapse it. Creativity relies on the urgency to look within for resonances, to feel our vulnerabilities and strengths, to let go of certainties and lift from our depths an intoxicating sobriety of self.

Stillness in Motion

A benefit of stillness is being able to feel what it is to be a body, to be able to be ourselves without the pressure of doing. No one else can do the job of living in our skin for us so we may as well strike up a lasting friendship. No need to hide. No need to get anxious or persnickety. No need to argue or offend. We need only connect to our muscle, skeleton, skin, breath, energy, motion, and emotion. We experience ourselves for ourselves and let be What Is. We perceive first hand our doing and our being. We feel the weight and mass of flesh that is us. We embody the ordinary and intricate details that comprise us and practice with the only body available, ours.

Sitting or lying still with awareness provides an opportunity to become intimate with the small motions of the body and any accompanying thoughts and emotions. The busyness of doing slows down enough for attention to rest in being. In coming to know stillness, we see what shows up on its own, often what's been there all along. We may feel the texture of our clothing rub against our skin. We may notice sadness or fear. We may notice sounds emanating from the intestines or from somewhere outside the room. We may notice not easily definable states, something dreamlike hovering like a cloud, an image appearing, then rapidly disappearing. Our senses wake up to the strands and waves of ourselves and the surroundings.

We let ourselves be curious. There are no distractions, only attractions. Notice what attracts attention, where it lingers and when it darts away. Rooting senses in the moment is a practice of being present, of feeling empowered, of establishing home in our body.

Rooting in the present and sensing small bodily motion may stir anxiety initially because of our unfamiliarity with being, inherited from a culture biased toward doing. The cultural norm often manifests as criticism of or discouragement in accepting What Is. What Is, we're told, is not enough—not that we give ourselves time to feel and get to know the contents and benefits of this moment. Instead cultural conditioning urges us toward doing more and doing better. Or the direction is reversed and we may judge ourselves as inadequate and resign ourselves to lethargy. Either way is a setup for discontent. Over time, a buildup of discontent contributes to a vicious cycle of disembodiment, angst, and anxiety.

That said, it's rare to meet anyone who is entirely anxiety free. Sipping tea on a lounge chair on the beach day after day, someone else tending to bills, dinner, and email—or whatever is your fantasy of ease—is an unrealistic ideal. It's more a matter of how much anxiety, how frequent, and what tools we use to lessen it. Certainly practicing stillness and somatically attuning without judgement to What Is challenges core beliefs. If still, are we doing, well, nothing? Is doing nothing okay? But this is precisely its point: to cultivate our ability to isolate a sensation, emotion, or behavior and identify how it's tied to notions that may or may not promote our best interests; to track it; to question assumptions and how they show up in our body and influence our movement and behavior; to release what no longer serves us and to ground awareness in the present. Look at how the hooks of culture and personal experience may have prevented us from living up to our potential. Pull them out of our flesh and find wound and salve and ingredients for creativity.

Practicing stillness and listening deeply are powerful, no session the same. Anxieties dissolve, fears and regrets lessen. As long as we're not practicing stillness on a sinking boat, oblivious to imminent danger, we discover safety and ease, an openness to What Is and its related opportunities, the ground solid beneath our feet. We connect with breath and renewing energy each moment.

The more we practice stillness, the more we notice. Says the poet Rumi about noticing the details, "Your deepest presence is in every small contracting/ and expanding,/ the two as beautifully balanced and coordinated/ as birds' wings."[3] Awareness refines to the point of detecting events that previously escaped attention like the ticking of a clock, a pinch in our hip, out inner eye witnessing colors wafting up like smoke. We witness whatever shows up: an itch, a strain, a sigh, thirst, thoughts about a past or future event, restlessness, and so forth. It's likely that we get carried off by a thought. So often living from our head, we are habituated to thinking. Sensing stillness, somatic attuning, is similar to meditation but with a difference. Meditation aims to quiet the mind and focus on the breath (or mantra or koan, depending on the meditation technique) with an aim, (depending on the tradition), toward experiencing what exists beyond mind. An example of this lies in the question for Zen practitioners, to discover one's original face prior to birth. Sensing stillness does not aim to surpass mind or achieve calm, although both are a likely result, but aims to notice isolated events and patterns of thoughts, emotions, sensations and movement. We notice. We notice which sense dominates and allow layers of being to reveal their secrets.

Practicing stillness parades both the noise and quiet of our minds. We watch the noise, our response to it, and where in our body it is felt. We watch, too, when the quiet arrives and the response to those periods, however long they last. Vipassana meditation teacher Jack Kornfield considers that stillness sacred. He says, "When you walk into a shaded grove of giant redwoods or into a great cathedral, a sacred stillness descends. As spaciousness opens within you, you can experience a profound silence in your very being.... This is the vast stillness that surrounds life. Trust it and rest in that stillness."[4]

Moving

As sacred as stillness can be, movement is a game changer. Movement alters the environment within our body. Movement stimulates the heart, breath, blood, brain, gut, energy, our proprioception on continual alert, situating and resituating the body on the move. There's no part of the body that sits out on the sidelines. We're not just in the game, we are the game. Bones and muscles flex, skin stretches, the nervous system and other systems activate. Balance is at stake. Bumping into a wall or a nearby person is at stake. Enzymes and hormones secreting is at stake. We participate in a visceral feedback loop, the body in motion, the body on alert to changes, our body on the go in process as process. We move the space of our body and the negative space around our body. As we move ourselves, we are moved. Move and discover a world already in motion and very much alive. Additionally, how we move influences what we sense and what we sense influences how we move.

Our body is not static. Technically "body" is a noun, but the somatically engaged person knows itself as a verb. We body the moment. We body motion. We body words. We body listening, sensing, feeling, and being. We embody. Constantly. We are motion and living processes incarnate, the flesh, water, air, atoms and cell of our matter in continual flux. In subtle and conspicuous ways, the body is always on the move. Our body is also interacting with fellow people, rocks, ferns, ponds, atoms, energy, and clouds.

Everything is alive. We are the heart and its beat. We are the stories drawn from the heart and memory, the ideas we identify with our head, the urges ignited from the gut, the impulses that arise from our trillions of cells and our electromagnetic field. We are our pelvis gyrating and shaking up vision. We are the increased sensitivity to floor or chair or air or cold. We are the memories stirred when we press against the wall. We are the stories we tell ourselves when we extend a leg backwards or believe that we can't due to poor balance. In a few minutes or hours, the sensitivity, stories, and memories may all shift as we move in another way, walk into the woods, climb a small hill, and sweat from the humidity and the exertion.

In choosing to move, we may do so to explore and pursue a physical inquiry. We move to see what hides in our flesh, to discover what stirs awake, what flushes our body with oxygen or a rush of blood, what motion lays a path for new neural connections. We do so for grace, insight, healing, and creativity. We move for relief from the push of doing and the pull of being, to honor the previously neglected, to feel how connecting more thoroughly to the fullness of our flesh connects us to what lies within and nearby. We find out how twisting is related to breathing which is related to elation which is related to how well or poorly we sleep at night. We find out how we wear the clothes and ideas of our culture and family and which fit better than others and which are best discarded. We find the emotional charge of yeses and the emotional charge of noes, which boundaries to maintain and which to loosen. We find out who emerges in motion, how we reveal our feminine and masculine qualities, and the benefit of integrating what is at odds with ourselves, be it boldness or reserve, or a desire to dance, journal, paint or garden. We find the matters of our flesh, the celebrated and tucked away, and the speed with which those matters appear or fade.

Movement establishes relationship. We cannot move one part of us without affecting the rest and unrest of us. The focus may be on lifting an arm but doing so requires moving a shoulder blade which is connected to the spine, an energy and nerve superhighway that is connected to delights and sorrows, the ability to lift a book or the decision not to. Every part of the body is connected to every other part of the body. Move one and all moves. Move the skeleton and muscles flinch. Curl the toes and our little building blocks of life, cells, signal fellow cells. Bend and an entire world bends with us.

The quality of the relationship to our body and surroundings, there all along, emerges into the foreground. We shift from experiencing ourselves as a head centered thought machine isolated in a unfeeling container into a moving, breathing, inspiring dynamic fleshy body in soulful alliance with fellow bodies and nearby life. We experience how the amount of pollutants in the air and the freshness of food influences stamina. We experience how the rhythms of the ocean, mountain, suburbs and city influences our heart beat. We experience how the presence of stress and delight activates cytoplasmic processes, the cellular soup of our body. Cell biologist Bruce Lipton identified those ingredients and mapped how thoughts and perceptions influence cellular health, ideas connected to epigenetics, the study of heritable changes in gene expression. Our DNA is not static as was previously thought, a scientific stance that carries profound implications. Says Lipton, "Signal transduction science recognizes that the fate and behavior of an organism is directly linked to its perception of the environment. In simple terms, the character of our life is based upon how we perceive it."[5]

How we perceive and how we move influences who we are and who we become. The thoughts and words and the stories we tell ourselves influences who we are and who we become. Our cells are listening. Our cells are continually paying attention.

It's unlikely that most of us feel cells activating, but we can notice our body contracting at encountering one thought and expanding with another. Perhaps the breath slows and deepens or a tremble arises. Perhaps we become dizzy or our hands heat up. We note our jaw clench or shoulders stiffen in response to someone's facial expression, a painting, a dance, a newspaper headline, a parent's hand reaching open palmed toward us. We notice what contributes to ease and what generates tension, what generates energy and what drains it, what ignites inspiration and what extinguishes the sparks. We learn what blocks the life pulse and what contributes to its flow.

Deliberate Embodiment

There is a significant difference between passive embodiment, our body absorbing and unconsciously reacting to its surrounding, and active, responsive embodiment, entailing a conscious witnessing, deciding how to respond, and determining new actions. It's impossible to not passively embody. Our senses are continually processing stimuli taking place regardless of our awareness. To be alive means to be impacted by family, school, the neighborhood, the weather, the order and disorder of our room, the politics of our job and of our country, whether we walk, drive, or bike to work, whether we feel free to express ourselves or guard expression. How we witness actions taking place, become conscious of stimuli, and then exercise choice is vital. We respond intentionally. We move intentionally. We do so to cultivate an integrated and flexible body. We move to embrace what matters and nourish the entirety of our being. We deliberately embody and affirm what nourishes the life pulse.

With deliberate embodiment, we create a structure for a physical inquiry. We pursue a somatic investigation to learn about our skin or breath or ribs or twitches or sadness. We employ our inner and outer senses and our proprioceptive and kinesthetic abilities to explore the world within and beyond our skin, within and beyond habitual motion and ideals. We look for signs of what buoys our life pulse and what weighs us down, the ephemeral signs and somatic insights that lead to acceptance and change. We look for how we dwell with our body, whether we stifle or free the life pulse, and align with the fertility of each moment.

It's impossible to determine all circumstances and control every motion and response. Life happens. The moon rises without our say. Flowers bloom without our say. What is within our control is how we greet circumstances. We choose our attitude. We choose a response. We choose our motion. Do we move with What Is or do we resist and look away? Better that we greet it with curiosity, feel somatic resonances, and consider each moment as an opportunity to learn. Better to access pliancy in the body for grounding and centering. The moon awaits our notice. The flowers welcome our attention. Our body prefers to rise to each occasion of breath and motion. It's up to us to listen to the body's cues, to probe more deeply and tend to the garden of our body.

How do we do that? Practice, practice, practice. It's up to each one of us to determine what is excessive and what is appropriate, what exhausts and what energizes, what heals and what hurts, what creates and what deteriorates. The distinctions can blur. Movement sharpens the focus and brings clarity. Movement articulates what may otherwise remain formless. Practice, yes, to find out how we respond.

Movement Approach: Flow and Impulse

In flow, the body awakens, loosens, stretches, inquires, pursues, and allows. It goes one direction and changes directions. It breathes deeply where it previously breathed shallow. The mind tests balance by alternating following with leading. The body first, then the mind. Or the mind first, then the body, eventually sensing their convergence, the two indistinguishable as bodymind. The gut cues up, the eye watching as a leg rediscovers strength and push or strength in yield. Arms cue up. Limb and muscle and bone fall into place. Gesture and pose, deepen and release. We allow. Welcome. Each impulse guides. We don't question flow, don't conceptualize. The body has its reasons and we abide by its currents. The unconscious lets down its guard. The ego puts down its pretenses. No type of motion or pattern reign supreme. All movements are welcome. All impulses. Specific direction or expectation is relaxed. Judgement is relaxed. The only rule is to keep moving and ride the tides.

There is no right or wrong, only motion, subtle and large, extending and contracting, scattered and orderly, athletic and meditative, awkward and graceful. Any combination rooted in the body. Connect to breath or heat or an object across the room or a moment's thought. Here is the body engaging in spontaneity, unplanned, uncoordinated, and gracing surprise.

Some questions worthy of pursuit:

- What is this moment asking of my body?
- What am I sensing?
- What sensation or thought or emotion hides behind an obvious movement?
- How can I move with the images and feelings showing up?
- What is authentic and natural, aligned to physiological rhythms?

Consider these questions before or after movement has ceased. Determine the best time to reflect. While moving, only move. While reflecting, only reflect. Then mix it up. Move like light or wind or thunder. Move from your cells or from the elongation of your spine. Move with the burden or blessing of work. Move as only you can move in this moment. Reflect from another perspective.

In flow, any impulse is worth pursuing, any motion worth doing, any doing worth unraveling, any being worth manifesting. Or not. We find out how alike and unalike we are from each other. Those who navigate with control may try a period with chaos. Those familiar with chaos might try a period with control.

Flow reveals and allows the body as process, body as motion, body in constant negotiation of inner and outer space. Allowing is valuable because we so infrequently indulge ourselves in letting the body roam and twist and still at will. A frequent result: Time becomes elastic. Ideas elasticize. Conceptualizing pauses. Move. Only move. Move some more. Any minute or sizeable movement is always the best movement. We pursue flow to be in flow and to relish presence, to step in and out of clarity, in and out of confidence, in and out of effort and delight. *(Exercise 3:4 Flow and Impulse)*

In flow, it is possible to experience reality as nondual. The usual separation between oneself and everything else disappears. We are motion. We are breath and heat. The usual hard borders of everything else soften. The lamp emanates energy. The floor emanates energy. The dog emanates energy. The emanating of everything dances with us in a blissful synchronic give and take that eventually blurs who and what is giving and who or what is taking. A relief stirs deep within the body that evades the precision of words.

To move in flow following impulses is among my greatest pleasures. I gladly release myself from the constraints of a chair and work obligations to let my body move on its own, abiding by no rules other than the joy of motion. I gladly engage myself physically, stretching arms and waist, twisting and lengthening. I follow the rhythm of music and of my own being. I don't need to determine consequent movements nor know where anything of them take me. Just move. Autotelic and impromptu, intoxicating and freeing, the accompanying joy is reason enough to move.

Flow is beneficial for experiencing the fluidity of one's boundaries, revealing intimate connectivity, what degree Other is us, our energy commingling with everything else. Flow helps us determine best practices, differentiating between unconscious reactive habits and actions done with our best interests in bodymind. Flow is thought in motion, embodied and malleable.

Movement Approach: Structure, Patterns and Actions

Contrasting flow is structure, the scaffolding that holds an experience in place, an organizational pattern. There is great benefit to having a structure that includes specific guidelines and limits. Such constraints provide a focus. It compels us to fit pieces into a whole as if solving a puzzle. It functions like a question which sets the pursuit of an answer into motion, an answer inherent in the questioning. Similarly, the structural constraint lays down a container for investigation.

A structure sets up a specific beginning and end. It puts forth an objective with steps along the way. It may include points to be reached, a pattern, repetitions. It may zigzag, undulate, parallel, rely on one side of the body or only one limb or region. The structure may rely on a specific place, a room or outdoor park, or dim or bright lighting.

I use the term "action" to depict a consciously constructed activity for exploration. An action includes an instruction with a set beginning and end and may be as simple as walking across the room with arms extended and heart soft and open. Another action could be to sit on a public bench and notice your reaction as various strangers sit beside you. Actions can be as simple or elaborate as wanted. An elaborate action may take place over several days or weeks and include other people. It may be artful, disruptive, or pleasing. It may be relational as is the previous example involving the park bench. You may consider plotting actions as in a story line. You might plan a few key scenes or activities and string them together intentionally.

The frame of the action sets the activity apart from other activities. Any activity can be an action but the frame compels us to consider the activity differently. We step out of usual activity into an activity that is somehow different, perhaps sublime. It is not life as usual but life as uncommon, our attention heightened, the moment peeling away layers of constructed meaning for something more personally consequential. We use the action is to investigate ourselves somatically and to heighten awareness. We use the action to turn mundane activity into something useful, insightful, transformative or any other objective that suits your needs and can stir your body awake. *(Exercise 3:5 Actions)*

Movement Approach: Speed and Unfamiliarity

The virtue of unfamiliarity is that it gets us to pay attention. It knocks out habitual approaches toward doing and perceiving and a tendency toward a lack of presence. Casual awareness is insufficient when circumstances change dramatically. Consider, for example, the difficulty in walking with a cast on our newly fractured foot as every sidewalk crevasse and inch of stair poses a potential obstacle. What was second nature, unworthy of our attention, now consumes complete attention. What was accomplished with grace has eroded into awkwardness and forced mindfulness. The greater challenge is to apply ongoing heightened attention to ordinary circumstances.

In awkwardness comes opportunities to examine and leave behind habits. In awkwardness comes learning through heightened attentiveness, activity broken down into manageable steps. What is taken for granted comes undone and opens a path for new awareness.

Changing speed is an effective way to increase attentiveness, to sense proprioceptively and kinesthetically or use any other neglected sense. Initially, slowing down may come across as boring and induce restlessness because so little seems to be happening. Stick with it long enough and a richness of detail shows itself. Which muscles, for instance, are activated to keep us standing? When we walk across the room, what part of us moves other than our legs? When we sit on the grass without gazing at our electronic devices or engaging in conversation, we may notice the blue jays, wrens, and squirrels, the softness of each blade of grass, the uneven earth supporting our haunches. Our mind often anxiously latches onto thought or an object for scrutiny. Much is taking place once noticing is enlisted and usual doing is halted. An activity is exposed as comprised of a myriad of tiny actions. We notice what was previously glossed over and the miraculous harmony that is needed to perform any activity.

Slowing down reveals texture, hue, and nuance. Slowing down reframes processes which reframes us. Slowing down challenges balance and centeredness. Or reinforces balance and centeredness. Slowing down gets us to realize what is missed when operating on auto pilot and what new horizons are reached upon re-employing the entirety of our body. Something as simple as slowly, very slowly lifting an arm to the chin reveals which muscles in the shoulder (expected) and which in the belly (unexpected) get engaged. Slowing down gives us time to recognize the expected and learn from the unexpected.

Speeding up also requires heightened awareness. Speed increases the risk of carelessness and injury. Speed can scatter attention, provoke dizziness and confusion. But it also excites the pump of adrenaline and a rhythm propelling us along to go further and further, pushing past unneeded boundaries into new territory. It pushes past our usual hesitation, doubts, or any other stall tactics. With a primary aim is to get words out, any words, mistakes and all, we may discover writing that what we ordinarily wouldn't have allowed, the rush having dislodged our usual inhibitions and criticisms. With the filters gone, our writing may experience its heyday. *(Exercise 3:5 Speed)*

Movement Approach: Breath

A body process often taken for granted is breathing. From the first moment we took air into our lungs as an infant, our lungs have been pulling in and expelling oxygen to ensure metabolism takes place and we remain alive. The lungs began their work at birth autonomically and have continued with minimal conscious input. We well know that the absence of breath leads quickly to our termination. Despite its paramount role, it's rare that we acknowledge and sense the particulars of our respiration.

Breathing is closely aligned with spirit and inspiration. "Breath" and "spirit" come from the same Latin word, "spiritus." The more deeply and smoothly we breath, the greater the chance of our spirited expression and inspiration. Our body fills and empties with this life-giving elixir, the cavity of the torso contracting and expanding in waves of motion. If these waves are restricted, the life pulse struggles and we fight for survival. When our breath is expansive, we enter the territory of beauty and bliss.

Breath is the entwining of mind with body and spirit with nature, all in alignment, all playing their vital role in the health of our flesh. Through breath, we seamlessly merge with the world beyond our body, one moment giving ourselves to the world, the next moment taking it in. Breathed air is the invisible river that quenches our rhythmic organismic thirst. Breath is the bridge and the shore, a renaissance of every moment. Breath is life's secret in the open.

When afraid, our breath temporarily halts. If stressed, the breath becomes shallow. If traumatized, the shallowness becomes a pattern. Deep, regular breath releases tensions, generates relaxation, and sustains the optimal hum of our body.

The patterns and quality of our breath influences mood, energy, thought and actions, and play a pivotal role in grounding and centering. Such knowledge is put to use during natural child birth, spiritual practices, and religious ceremonies to generate an altered state. With its vital role in well-being and expression, it helps to recognize the details of our personal breath and harness its power. (*Exercise 3:7 Sending Breath to Relax*)

Movement Approach: Emotion and Sensation

In previous chapters, I've mentioned the importance of noticing emotions as physiological events when they arise. Depending on the situation, we likely hold back or express emotions, cultural as well as family and group norms determining their degree of appropriateness. Emotions are complex neural activities involving all parts of the brain. Emotions are the affective ways we respond to a situation. Psychiatry professor Daniel Siegel acknowledges much disagreement as to their definition. While researching for one of his books, he concluded: "No one seemed to have a commonly shared view of what emotions really were beyond descriptions of their characteristics."[6] He explains that an anthropologist sees emotions as a cultural link across generations, sociologists say they are what holds people together, and neurologists see them as the link between the brain and the body.

What we can agree to is that they motivate or hinder us, providing the impetus to take action or do nothing. They are tied to our ability to respond in ways that enable us to survive. They move us toward nourishment and safety and away from danger. For these reasons we owe them a debt; they lead the way. They are evidence of our responsiveness. Our emotions create a state of consciousness and physiological conditions which in turn influences perceptions and motion. Consider the boiling of blood, hormones in a rush, at the instigation of anger. Often we feel conflicted by emotions categorized as negative such as anger or jealousy and welcome positive emotions such as love and joy. We may struggle with which best to listen to, passion or reason, no guarantee that one will win out over the other. We prefer to be in control of them rather than they with us. We don't always get our way.

Interestingly, the word "emotion" contains motion. Implied in every emotion is movement. With the arrival of emotion, the body is moving. The association isn't one that first comes to mind, especially since we source all emotion with the heart, yet emotion is a full body affair.

In close alliance to emotion is sensation. Sensation is similarly a physiological response but typically without the affective charge. Sensation gets into the stickiness of language. While there are differences, there are also huge similarities between, for instance, physical and emotional pain. Both can generate distress and both can feel vague, a reason doctors often ask patients to describe pain on a 1 to 10 scale. Interestingly, there is a huge overlap in the brain as to the areas that light up when we experience physical or emotional pain.

Locating and identifying emotions and sensations in the body shows us to what degree we are embodied. Do we separate ourselves, even become numb, or do we find them the intimate link to inhabiting ourselves? Sometimes, numbing out and dissociating is the best way to deal with unbearable pain, the nervous system overload, the body shutting down as a method of coping. But it becomes problematic if our initially helpful response freezes us in a habitual defense pattern long after the precipitating event or events have ended.

Because emotions and sensations fall somewhere on the pleasure/pain continuum, judged either by us or a larger social body, we don't always have an impartial perception of them. Our judgement or thinking about them divides us from feeling our body. When we finally let go of judgements, an entire world of sensory detail reveals itself. Extreme emotions are impossible to miss. Anger, for instance, feels like a raging wildfire, the body adrenalized, sensation beginning perhaps at the chest before the rest of the body is consumed. But if the anger is judged as bad or shameful, the feelings tend to go underground which means they could appear when we least expect them or influence other behavior without our knowing.

With attention, the more subtle emotions and sensations come forth, there all along, ready to inform us. What does a slight burn in the back of the neck indicate? Why has our ankle, all of a sudden, seem less capable of supporting our weight? As attention is engaged and we become more somatically literate, we come to know the motion of our emotions. With awareness comes choice, insight, healing, and wisdom. We feel their connection to our life pulse. We come to know ourselves. We feel how we move and what moves us.

Movement Approach: A Miscellany of Ideas

Operating both behind the scenes and in full view, emotions play a significant role in how we move. Using emotions for a physical inquiry is bound to uncover habits and can lead to insights and a new range of motion. There are countless approaches to movement. Below are several to apply for a movement exploration:

- Move only the upper, lower, right, left or a specific part of your body.
- Rely on only one system to move: skeletal, muscular, glandular, nervous.
- Wear a blindfold while moving.
- Say yes to every impulse.
- Shift awareness and originating impulses back and forth between the interior and exterior of the body.
- Vary the quality of movement such as fluid, staccato, forceful, and lyrical.
- Sit, stand, or lay on the floor to change altitude.
- Use props.
- Engage negative and positive space.
- Create a short sequence of movements and repeat them with and without variations.
- Challenge balance.
- Be still.

Movement Habits and Expansion

We engage in movement every day. Familiar actions involving movement include brushing teeth, lifting a fork and spoon, getting into the front or back seat of a car, and crossing the street. The number of familiar daily actions, each a series of movements that can be broken down into smaller units of motion, is lengthy. These familiar actions are carried out for their functionality. We learn how to perform them with a comfortable efficiency, then rarely give them a second thought, all of which comes in handy in tending to daily routines. Minimal somatic awareness is needed, our attention often split between the action and something else. While crossing the street, rather than notice our feet strike the pavement or the whoosh of a passing car against our skin, we may be thinking about the meeting about to take place. These types of actions are pedestrian, that is, they are quotidian movements that scant receive a second thought.

Many of these actions and the specific movements are derived from culture. The culture determines what is or is not acceptable. For instance, some cities are indifferent to someone jaywalking and dashing across the street whereas another city scoffs at such actions, preferring, even installing electric signs that determine when it is appropriate to cross at the corner. So serious is jaywalking that some jurisdictions classify it a misdemeanor. Another example are cultures such as Korea that encourage sitting on the floor, your age and gender determining how you cross your legs and the height, if any, of your cushion.

Among culturally determined situations that fascinate me are the scripted movements that takes place in elevators, a reason why a few of my performances have taken place in an elevator or an elevator was created for a stage. In the former, well aware that common elevator movement is to be stationary, certainly not dancing, I continually went up and down in a public elevator while tangoing with a partner. (One of the fellow occupants alerted security who eventually arrived to request my partner and I vacate the elevator.) In the performance on stage, every time the door opened, a troupe and I held a posture that pointed at unacceptable activity taking place when the doors shut, such as leaning against each other. Common, socially acceptable elevator behavior includes standing still facing the door and silently awaiting your floor. Fellow occupants will eye you unkindly if you sit on the floor, face a wall other than the door, or, as happened with me, dance between floors.

In the privacy of our home, we similar subscribe to familiar, acceptable movements. We sit on chairs, lie on beds, walk across doorways, and limit the range of our motion vocabulary due to conventions. Most adults do not leap on couches, drape ourselves off the bed or down the stairs, and lie across doorways. Such actions are more common to children.

Expand, I say, on possibilities. Consider the movements you do and how your do them. Turn commonplace activity into an action. Use activity to refine awareness. Increase your expressive range in subtle and emboldened ways. Welcome the enlivening that comes from broadening the range of motion. Explore the difference between functional movement and expressive movement. Explore the difference between routine, habituated and disembodied movement and impromptu, inspired, and embodied movement. Uncover what it means to more fully inhabit your flesh.

In stillness and in motion, we come to better know our embodied, experiential truths. In stillness and motion, we find a world awaiting us.

Go, I say, move your body. Let yourself be moved. Discover what takes place when you open to motion, when you listen deeply to what occurs when your body lifts up from your chair. Do so with attentiveness. Cross the room in a few or many steps. Pause along the way to notice what comes into view. Listen deeply. From the other side of the room, find a new vantage point and a new perspective. Find the sacredness of stillness and of motion.

Exercises

3:1 Simple Warmup

- Stand.
- As you stand, feel how the floor supports your feet and legs, assisting you in standing upright. Feel the solidity of the floor. Spread and wiggle your toes. Shift your weight from the heel of your feet to your toes. Repeat this a few times. Imagine you are widening the soles of your feet and a root is reaching from the arches of your feet into the floor and the ground below.
- Know there is no right or wrong way to do this. Notice what you notice. Follow your attention and the subtle movements of your body.
- Shift your weight onto your left foot, then your right. Rock from left to right. Go slowly. Notice how your weight pours down one leg, then the other.
- Loosen your knees. Allow them to have some give, a small bend that reinforces balance.
- Imagine your spine. Beginning with your tail bone, extend your spine upward like a stem unfurling in the morning sun. Invite new space, additional cushion between each vertebrae. Softly rise upward. Notice any changes in your breath. Welcome yawns.
- Make small circles with your shoulders. Go slow. Do five circles. The slower pace encourages ignored muscles to engage and habits to shift. Again, notice what you notice. There may be heat or coolness, tingles or strain. Just notice. Reverse the direction of the circle for five repetitions.
- Rotate your head to the right while keeping your chest forward. Go a tad further. Look over the shoulder by moving only your eyes. Do the same on the left before returning your gaze forward.
- Be sure your feet are still rooted to the floor. Tilt your head downward, chin angled or touching your chest, and gently roll your spine downward, letting the weight of your head, then shoulders, pull you toward the floor. Go as far as is comfortable, your knees loose. At the point where you can go no further, rest there by taking two complete breaths, before slowly rolling back up.
- Rest in standing. Root your feet rooted. Elongate your spine. Enjoy easy breathing.

3:2 Doing and Being Exercise

- Movement: Come up with a Doing movement. Make it something simple like moving a chair to another location in the room. Do it slower than you might otherwise. What do you notice?
- Switch to Being. Using the same Doing action. If you chose to move the chair, position yourself at the chair and pause to check in with your senses. Wait until an impulse arises to act before following through. Pause again and wait for an impulse to follow through on. Repeat at least 3 times.
- How would you describe the differences between the approaches?
- Writing: Come up with a brief writing with a Doing focus. Keep it simple. Perhaps write a paragraph about your first pet or the design of your car. What stops, flows and sensations do you notice during the writing?
- Switch to Being: Wait until a word or phrase compels you to write. Then continue in stream of consciousness. Allow whatever writing arises take to take place.
- How would you describe the differences between these approaches? What purpose might they each have for you?

3:3 Body Scan Exercise

- Sit comfortably or lay down.
- Beginning with your head, scan your head for any sensations taking place. If you find something, make a mental note. You can also scan specific parts of your head: forehead, eyes, nose, mouth, ears. As you scan, ground your entire body.
- Scan your neck for any sensations taking place.
- Continue to scan the entire body: shoulders, upper chest, heart, lungs, liver, spleen, stomach, intestines, shoulders, arms, hands, pelvis, ovaries/testes, genitals, thighs, knees, calves, ankles, feet. Linger at a region if it warrants attention. Check with your breath regularly to ensure ease.
- What areas did you notice sensation or any other activity?
- How would you describe that activity? Write the details of that activity.

3:4 Exercise: Flow and Impulse

- Select ambient music if wanted. Sit on the floor, lay down, or stand. Set a timer for 15 minutes.
- Begin to move. Start anywhere—feet, hands, neck, belly. Slide across or root into the floor. Gently undulate or extend limbs sharply. Keep moving no matter what. Move without knowing why. Let the smallest motion enlarge.

Repeat movements. Go slow or quickly. Move from bone or muscle. Any movement is the right movement. Move continuously.
- If unsure what to do next shows up, find the tiny movements the body is already doing. Exaggerate and vary them. Do any movement. Snap fingers. Wave at the wall with your hands and your entire body.
- Consider bold movements and incremental movements. Take up lots of space or a small area. Let warmth or image or memory or sensation lead. Let curiosity or uneasiness or another quality carry you forth. Stay with one type of movement or switch innumerable times. Be a river or a trickle.
- Pursue any impulse that shows up. Allow what wants to come forth to come forth. Allow what wants to hide to remain hidden. Let be what wants to be. There is no wrong way to do this. Your way is your way.
- Upon completion, notice where you feel the residue of your actions.

Exercise 3:5 Actions

Any activity can be an action. The ones below are ordinary activity. Feel free to come up with your own, as simple or complicated as wanted. Decide when the action begins and when it ends.

3:5:1 Getting a Drink of Water

- Retrieve a glass of water. What does water represent for you? Notice your movement as you approach the water.
- Pour yourself a glass. Notice how you hold the glass. What do you normally take for granted?
- Drink. Notice how the water fills and exits your mouth. What does it feel like? What, if any changes do you notice?
- Does water or drinking stir any memories?
- Write about what you notice.

3:5:2 Folding Down to the Floor

- Beginning from standing, very slowly bend down to the floor.
- What muscles are used? Is your balance impacted? How easy or difficult is this to do?
- Stand up and slowly bend down again, only this time, fold down. What changes?
- Repeat folding down in a variety of ways. Which ways make you feel strong or weak? If you get dizzy, where do you experience it? What emotions

arise in either the downward or upward motion? Do you prefer to be up or down and why?
- Write about what you notice.

3:5:3 Taking Out the Garbage

- Go to one of the trash containers nearby.
- Peer at its contents, each item once a part of your or another's life.
- Walk it to the container that gets taken by a trash collector. Given that these items are one step further from your life, what thoughts, memories, or sensations are elicited?
- Dump the contents. Notice what you notice.
- Write about what you notice.

3:6 Exercise: Speed and Unfamiliarity

- Slowing Down: Sit on the floor or a chair. In slothfully slow motion, rise up to standing. Take more time than ever to complete the action. Notice what you notice.
- Do the same with any other ordinary action.
- What do you notice that escaped your usual attention? How did slowing down reveal? How did it challenge you?
- Speeding Up: Come up with four motions such as lifting your left leg, turning your head to the right, frowning, and extending your arms. Repeat these motions as rapidly as possible. Try to maintain the integrity and completeness of the motions. What did the speed reveal? How did it challenge you?
- What appealed to you each speed?

3:7 Sending Breath to Relax

- Lie on your back in a comfortable position. Let your weight fall against the surface.
- Follow the patterns of your breath. Your breathing may initially be labored. Wait for it to return to normal. Turn your attention to sensation at your ribs, shoulder blades, and belly. Let your breath do what it wants.
- Once you become acquainted with your breath, turn your attention to an area of tension. Invite breath to that area. Imagine your lungs capable of sending breath anywhere you intend it to travel. Imagine that tense area embracing the replenishing air. Repeat this several times.
- Move on to another tense area.
- Upon completion, inhale and exhale deeply. If you feel sleepy, enjoy a nap.

4

The Verbal Body

In response to an assignment in fourth grade, I wrote a story set in Austria about a fir tree. I'd never been to Austria, knew scant little about fir trees, yet the students believed my every word and refused to accept the story as fiction. Theirs and my teacher's response launched an interest in and recognition of the power of writing. Limited movement due to my doctor's unwise advice concerning my scoliosis furthered that interest in high school. My unmoving body craved relief from physical pain and pent up emotions. I turned to writing. I turned to what was available. The writing provided an expressive outlet and gave my skin permission to speak. But it wasn't until college and the introduction of motion into my expressive repertoire that I more fully inhabited my body and my words. No longer casting off pain and disembodying, I embraced my discomfort, stiffness, and spasms. As my muscles strengthened and adopted greater flexibility, my writing stretched and opened. The prison of my spinal condition became the path to freedom.

The movement of words tied to my body shifted my restrictions into lubrication and mobility. In every poem, story, and journal entry, expression and understanding bloomed beyond the bind of simple impressions. Every time I opened the blank page, hazy details of my life came into focus, emotional bumps came to the fore and soothed, and my bodymind wiped a thin layer of crud from its eyes. A single word, like the resonant strike of a drum, connected me to the flesh home of my body and to new realizations. Each phrase and page pointed toward and manifested possibility.

A power of writing is its viscerality. The addition of movement and somatic awareness heightens the body and word connection. The body wants to share its verbal urges and to tell its stories. It wants to be acknowledged, to be heard, to lay itself on the line. Referring to writing's impact upon him, travel writer Pico Iyer who practices stillness for embodiment says,

> To write is to step away from the clamor of the world, to take a deep breath and then, slowly and often with shaking heart, to try to make sense of the bombardment of feelings, impressions, and experiences that every day and lifetime brings. The very act of putting them

4. The Verbal Body

down—getting them out of the beehive of the head and onto the objective reality of paper—is a form of clarification. And as the words begin to take shape and make pairings across the page, gradually you can see what you thought, or discern a pattern in the random responses.[1]

Writing is sensing incarnate. Writing helps make sense. Writing communicates to us as we engage in the activity and to a wider audience, if the writing is made public. It helps with clarity, creating patterns and order, changing us along the way. Its expression is the voice made visible, the still silent body made audible and fluid. The body as process fleshes out.

Words are felt bodily presences. They take up residence in our connective tissue, in the inner sanctum of our cells and the rapid fire of neurons. They await our grasp and their play upon the page. They await our writing, our consideration and gaze. They want to be touched by writing and partake in one form becoming another form, a flesh body shedding a skin for a text body.

Writing moves us. Writing writes us. The writing shows us who we are. We honor the voice of our body, the language created from tongue and breath and heart and gut. The writing is an intelligence or awareness channel to refine our sensing and engage with the world. Likening writing to a way to journey through our life, dancer and poet Celeste Snowber says, "This would be a good travel plan: bring the body home to language. An all inclusive excursion where the body infiltrates the way we write, speak, and even think."[2]

Writing words as felt presences

Writing places us in our body, helping us to feel less separate from ourselves and from others. The lines carry us away and pull us inward. The lines say what we need to read. They generate a dialog, a form outside us, a rapid transit to the heart of our matter. Writing gets us developing a language of listening to the well-chosen word that strikes at meaning and purpose, a resonance that places us in harmony with the bones and breath of our being.

Moving Resonant Writing

The critical ingredient that separates the somatic process discussed in this book from other somatic techniques is its inclusion of the importance of writing. The two practices work hand in hand to further embodiment. Though the field of somatics has grown in the last several decades with the development of more techniques and licensed practitioners applying findings and techniques to fields as diverse as dance and leadership, still lacking is an appreciation of somatically inspired writing along with fitting expression for writing about the moving body.

Somatic practitioners and dance writers frequently express frustration with the imprecision and abstractedness of writing. In this scenario, words fall short of their mark. They are deemed too abstract, engaged in an impersonal objective linguistic system with no connection to a personal body. Writing is fated to fail at capturing the subjective experience of the flesh, even in expert hands who can turn phrases with astounding finesse. The body's visceral immediacy with all its nuances gets lost to the abstractions and clunkiness of writing. The body dwells in the moment, thrives in sensual engagement, each limb and sensory cue pulsing with the vitality of presence. Its subtleties are endless. Writing, too often, is distant, inexact, disorienting, disembodying, experience and sensual involvement a fading memory that we desperately try to resurrect. Writing gets us to lose touch with What Is. Presence loses its luster as focus narrows upon thought that is devoid of a somatic self. The body takes a back seat, eventually falling into a slumber that reawakens only upon physical activity or the gulp of hefty shots of espresso.

Sometimes.

It depends on who is doing the writing and how the writing is approached.

Sometimes writing is clunky, imprecise, an approximation of an experience, the actual experience as evasive as a morning's rapidly evanescing dream. Sometimes writing is devoid of a body—any body. Sometimes writing cloaks itself in the garments of the authoritative privilege of objectivity. This type of writing with its subject-verb-object conventions has its place. It's essential to the sciences, to aeronautics, oceanography, and encyclopedias to name only a few. It's essential for optimizing effective communication across groups of diverse people with a range of educational and social backgrounds.

It is not the type of writing promoted in these pages. The writing promoted here supports somatic writing. The type of writing promoted here, a writing from the body, recognizes the power of resonance. Resonant writing aligns us with the idiosyncratic rhythms, energy, images, sayings, idiolects and felt presences of our personal body. It supports deep listening. It reaches places where the moving body hints at and may be unable to go alone. It lets us ride the waves of verbal expression in unison with the breath and breadth of our personal body to generate meaning, healing, creativity, and integrative awareness. It helps in the process of embodying. It personalizes the objectivity of language and connects us to the nature of our expression. It gets us to articulate what may otherwise be ignored. It praises deeply embodied cognition, our body our own, our body ripe with the fruit of its motion, emotion, clues and wisdom. We may separate mind from body or writing from moving, but the division, only temporary, is en route to a more integrated whole, neurons passing from one hemisphere of the brain to the other, new paths for awareness laid down with every turn of phrase.

How we connect to writing matters. Do we frame it a staid system created by literate ancestors or recognize it as a living system that relies on our usage to keep it alive and meaningful? Yes, there is a lexicon to draw from along with standards of grammar, syntax, and mechanics, but we use the rules and bend them to make the writing our own. We let the writing speak us in the way that only an individual body can. We find our body through textualizing and contextualizing ourselves. We find that words and phrases emanate meaning and set up residencies in our body.

By themselves, movement and writing are powerful languages. Movement is often considered to be the closest and most intimate expression of our being. The history of every one of our life events is written into our flesh, imprinted upon our tissues and cells, our blood and bone, the very fabric of our being. Conscious and unconscious movements reveal this history, blazoned in our flesh and motion, readable to those with a discerning eye. It's no wonder that dancer Martha Graham said, "Movement does not lie."[3] How we move, our flexibility, strength, speed, and vibrancy are clues. Movement appeals because its visceral immediacy touches into and accesses the multitude of these conscious and unconscious experiences, providing a direct link to our life pulse.

Writing is equally powerful. Stringing words together, verbs pressing against nouns, adjectives and adverbs vying for space, a comma here and there, a period following soon after. Writing is a defining, expressive, and meaning-making act. The pursuit and ordering of words frames experience and establishes an opportunity for reflection and understanding. Each word points to the shape of experience. Writing is a path of knowing, a process of cognition, an act of being and becoming. The flesh gives voice to sing or rant, a verbal dance of cells, atoms, energy, intention, and attention.

Many understandably stay away from writing. Critical of their ability to devote words to page, they are writing avoidant. Can't spell, can't construct a sentence, no ideas worth writing are among their reasons. Scarred by the red pen of school which taught a type of writing that excluded somatic awareness, students were often guided to fit their personal expression into book reports and essays, ready-made structures that neglected individual and idiosyncratic verbal paths. Many schools omitted expressive creative writing as unnecessary, except as an elective at best. With writing commonly taught to conform to objective standards, it neglected its power to foster growth, empathy, creative expression, healing, imagination, and integration. The unfortunate result from relying on a singular approach to writing is that many of us too often assess our skills as inferior. Our enthusiasm never developed. Why write? Why pursue a difficult activity that reaps meaningless rewards? Why not find a more worthwhile and satisfying pursuit like hiking or playing soccer?

Omitting a writing practice quashes and silences our voice before we know its sound, snuffing its magic before its flame illuminates our inner and outer worlds. Without writing, we may unwittingly block its route to new vistas, surrendering a perceptual path whose benefits we may never learn. Ignorance is bliss until we know otherwise. Our knowing changes once we experience the power and satisfaction that comes with connecting to a truth of our body through verbal expression that liberates, relieves, and affirms us. We discover writing as viscerally authentic and meaningful. We discover that, like moving, it leads us to recognize What Is, to embody presence and manifest the life pulse.

The life pulse is strengthened through releasing the voice, in writing what needs to be said, in revealing what we dare, what we dream, hope, and fear, in cultivating the imagination, in connecting to the ephemeral phenomenon of our felt body, and putting ourselves word after word on the line. Writing is the flesh made word, the breath shaped and refined, the morass of our thoughts, feelings, and sensations clarified. Writing is a point or line of focus, a series of sounds and images lining a path. Writing is a way of being. We write to confide, to connect to our personal body, to reinforce presence, to share the shape and sound of our voice as it resonates, quivers, and pulses with life, to connect to our flesh and to the heart and mind of others. We write to find out what is known and what is yet to be known, to vision and birth possibilities.

Those with a writing practice testify to its need and power to uplift. Says writer Audre Lourde about poetry, "[It] is not a luxury. It is a vital necessity of our existence. It forms the quality of the light within which we predicate our hopes and dreams toward survival and change, first made into language, then into idea, then into more tangible action. Poetry is the way we help give name to the nameless so it can be thought."[4] She speaks about poetry, however her ideas holds true for other forms of writing as well.

Writing externalizes feelings and ideas considered internal. It is a meeting point between the external and internal world, a bridge from what you sense to what you say, from what you don't know to what you do, a path that leads directly to you and points out the forest, the bees, your neighbor, and the stream. We take the language not originally self made, its grammar, mechanics, and vocabulary, and make it our own, somatically connected to the flesh of our body.

Somatic Writing Approach

Unlike moving which we do daily, most of us do not write with any regularity—aside from a brief electronic missive. Surrounded by words heard and spoken as soon as we wake up each morning, we might assume writing would come easily. But writing is a peculiar balancing act of great assertiveness and great passivity, both an effort and a letting go. Many of us, already disembodied, write from a similar stance, the body a remote influence upon the text which is a collection of letters abiding by rules agreed upon before our birth and indifferent to our influence. An embodied somatic writing perspective recognizes those rules as malleable and working in our behalf, a relationship of mutuality and authenticity. The writing rises up, a natural occurrence. It shows up the way it shows up. Its forming reflects our forming, a mutual reverberation.

Writing halts our usual doings to assemble letters into words, words into sentences, sentences into blocks of text, all intended to convey experience. Depending on the approach, writing could lean toward an act of doing, an act of being, or a combination of both. Writing may prove a point and be a deliberate, predetermined orchestration of ideas toward a foregone conclusion. Or it may have no predetermined plan and conclusion, the knowing revealing itself in the process of writing. It may be a verbal stream winding its way around rocks and fallen branches, word after written word their own reason for being. In *Agua Viva*, writer Clarice Lispector embraces the moment and says, "I don't know what I'm writing about: I am obscure to myself. I only had initially a lunar and lucid vision, and so I plucked for myself the instant before it died and perpetually dies. This is not a message of ideas that I am transmitting to you but an instinctive ecstasy of whatever is hidden in nature and that I foretell. And this is a feast of words."[5]

The writing may function on multiple levels at the same time, a concurrence of being and doing, a catalyst reaching new thought and feeling, a narrative that follows its own inherent logic, an expression of the previously unseen, a sleek winged glider skimming clouds to unobstructed sky. The writing may be literal, energetic, psychological, spiritual, metaphoric, euphoric, or evolutionary. It may be instructive, destructive, descriptive, provocative, or protective. It may contain lengthy alliteration and rhymes or be short, astute, with no discernible pattern. It can be used to solve a problem, explain, describe, tell a story, embody, exclaim, or offer insight. This list, far from comprehensive, is intended to get us to veer away from traditional categories for framing experiences such as fiction, nonfiction, and poetry. The idea, rather, is to language ourselves, to open to verbal possibilities, to let writing take us to an utterable form. Let our body speak. Let our body write itself. Let each phrase remind the body of its phrases of being and return us to the home of our flesh. *(Exercise 4: 1 Defining Writing)*

With any writing, prompts help. They provide a topic, method, structure, or throughway to spur writing. They open the writing channel and provide a container to hold and shape the material. Common approaches include identifying emotions and ideas and following a formal outline. Other approaches rely on narrative, a central image, mood, or defining a character and voice. Any prompt or prop that inspires writing and keeps the words coming is a good one. Whatever propels a generative verbal flow is worthwhile.

Somatic writing is based on sensing how words and phrases reside in the body in stillness and in motion and tuning into their innate rhythms and perceptions. Somatic writing uses the objective system of grammar, mechanics, and sentence formation while also connecting to the somatic body with all its fleshy impressions, truths, and contradictions. The writing originates from any region—or the entirety—of our connective tissue and the collision of inner and outer worlds. The writing rises up from our matter and breath, our energy and the resonance of words, the felt presences that inhabit us. The writing is a dialog with ourselves and, if wanted, with an audience. The writing is an inquiry into and representation of embodiment, a discursive journey into sound, breath, image, and vibration, a verbal representation of being.

Pairing writing to somatic awareness is a rare combination but herein lies its strength: writing furthers the understanding, expression, awareness of the somatic body which, in turn, furthers the expressive capability of writing. The focus on our personal body with its specific history, behaviors, perceptions, rhythms, and expression recorded in our flesh is the prima materia for writing. Where words go, so follows the body. Where the body is, so goes the words. The combination shakes up the usual divide between mind and body and positions writing as unifier and transformer. Simultaneously, the definition and experience of our bodymind expands and fleshes out.

Writing brings to the line what the flesh carries in wordless quiet, drawing from the unconscious and the conscious, from the murmurs and half told tales and expression folded into our flesh. With the attention, our body speaks its mind through every twist of the tongue and phrase and phase of being. Writing and body pair up as carriers of energy, as conveyors of the life pulse.

Resonant writing requires tuning in somatically to notice the felt impact of words and phrases. Where in the body do they resonate? Where do they rise up or land? How long do they remain in one place before traveling? We consider their sound, meaning, or any other part of the words. Going beyond known sites like the heart and head and familiar emotional responses reveals new information and supports the life pulse. Words, we discover, are living beings, shadows that slip into light, tremors that loosen the imagination, sherpas that carry our burdens and lead us through difficult life passages. Initially the process may challenge our assumptions about writing and language, but practice eventually exposes the dynamic connection between our body and our writing.

Writing Approach: Resonance

Resonant writing is based on the premise that words impress upon and dwell within with a reverberating energy. Words are messengers from nearby or afar driven to deliver a communication. They contain ideas and images, disturbances and delights, questions and affirmations. They dwell ephemerally in us as energy and shape shifters influencing our body. They may be a composite of any number of elements: fragmented impressions, clouds of emotions, memories tied to geography or time, a combustion of cells respiring, the glow of love, the stress of work, an ease of breath after a bout of

Reflecting on resonance

asthma. Amorphous at first, these phenomena coagulate into words, as recognizable, visible and audible manifestation of hidden workings of our body.

Words carry associations. For instance, from a young age, I had difficulty pronouncing "aluminum," the m and n tripping my mouth. I added extra syllables as collateral damage, a full on mangle of elocution. My tongue's rapid dart between my teeth, lips pursing, upper palate closing upon the lower palate provoked laughter not just once, but from many failed attempts. I can say the word now, but not without a quiver in my lower lip.

We may have favorite words associated with meaning. In response to an interviewer's question about her favorite word, novelist Margaret Atwood replied, "And. It is so hopeful."[6] Where, I'd follow up, do you feel the sensation of "and?" Where does hope live in your body? Locating words and identifying characteristics of that location can release a host of information about us. What previously was ignored gets defined, recognized, understood. It provides an entry into the mystery of our body. It shows the flight of words and how they land. It shows how words move through us. *(Exercise 4:2 Resonance)*

Writing Approach: Pacing

A critical component of somatically informed writing is speed. The pace of writing lets us switch attention back and forth between awareness of the page and awareness of our body as words resonates within. The pace allows us to determine what speed best supports embodied writing.

Fast unleashes a torrent of words which lubricates the writing muscle. The idea is to continue placing words on the page no matter what. No judgement and no correcting. Just an ongoing verbal stream rushing out. Fast pushes past hesitancy and doubt. Fast mixes careless with carefree. Both are welcome. Both honor the stream and the manifestation of the life pulse. There is no need to second guess or correct. First words on the page stay on the page. They may trip over themselves into nonsensical nomenclature, a repetition of syllables and words going nowhere, or glide confidently across the page like a rowing team, every word and motion synchronized for grace and strength and confluence with creative currents.

Fast may lead to an obvious awareness of the body such as a strain of the wrist or shoulder and necessitate adjusting our position. We notice what promotes tension and what promotes ease. What else rises up in the wake of fast?

Slow provides a luxury of time for exploration. Slow encourages writing a few words, then switching attention toward the body to find a response. The response may be subtle, perhaps a flutter or another momentary sensation that you may think imaginary. Stick with the finding anyway. This is the path of learning to read our somatic signals and developing somatic literacy. Once we've found a response, attention returns to the page for more writing. We can continue the sentence or topic previously begun, start anew, or write about our bodily finding. Back and forth, page to body attention goes.

Both speeds yield somatic findings, to writing, and to discovering how words live in us. Both reinforce embodied writing. Depending on the sought after result, practice determines a pace that unifies the body of the text with the body of writing. *(Exercise 4:3 Pacing)*

Writing Approach: Rhythm

Every phrase of writing and every phrase of movement or stillness illuminates each other. They work hand in hand, a collaboration of consciousness and unconsciousness, of imprinting and expressing, of flesh and text. The process of alternating attention between body and page during writing lights up multiple areas of the brain, a neuronal ricochet that heightens perceptions and furthers expression. We make connections. Words are not empty and abstract, adrift in a void, but rooted in the connective tissue of body and life energy. The body is experienced as a vitally responsive instrument in dialog with itself and the environment. It's up to us to awaken to our verbal relationship, to establish a personal felt connection between word and flesh and to articulate our embodied senses and inherent wisdom.

Somatic writing drawn from the head, heart, gut, the motion of the limbs, essentially everywhere that emotion and thought embed themselves, rides on our physical being and bioelectrical currents. Novelist Paul Auster recognizes the source. He says, "Writing is physical for me. I always have the sense that the words are coming out of my body, not just my mind. I write in longhand, and the pen is scratching the words onto the page. I can even hear the words being written.... There's something about the rhythms of language that correspond to the rhythms of our own bodies."[7]

Somatically generated writing grounds us in our individual body. It reveals our personal rhythms, images, and voice informed by the stories, themes, and impressions of our life. Among its strengths, it distinguishes what makes us unique. We cannot be duplicated verbatim. Another may adopt our rhythms but the fit is always imperfect.

The rhythm roots us in our personal self, forming and informing us. Rhythmic writing aligns with the timing of our personal body, the heartbeat, the blood pulse, the ultradian rhythms that prompts the hourly release of hormones, and longer infradian rhythms that influence functions like menstruation. It acknowledges that there are natural body patterns. In contrast, arrhythmic writing, like entries in an encyclopedia, tends toward factual monotony that minimizes a personal body and puts forth a facade of impersonal, objective authority.

Rhythm is a unifier. Its tempo creates patterns and sensuous phrasing, a music easily grasped by the body that prefers connection because it is itself rhythmic. The rhythms in the writing reflect and support the life pulse. Writing with a rhythm can feel exalting and transcendent because we are touching deeply into subjective, affective, nuanced experiences. We are both concentrating on putting ourselves on the line and expanding. We are allowing being. The moment to moment mystery of our subcutaneous body is given voice, vision, breath, and motion. Word by word and line after line with an inherent momentum and perhaps its own logic, our usual push toward doing relaxes into reprieve. As both a guide in the process and a curious bystander, the writing propels us ahead. We engage verbal being, letting ourselves go yet held into form by the page, our life on the line.

Rhythm connects us to the felt experience of our biology, secreting, beating, and pulsing in accord with rhythms much larger than our personal body. We are the writer and the written, akin to the difference between the dancer and the dance, the mover and the moved. We are not alienated from the biology of our nature or nature in general, but its very waves, the flow of our words in confluence with the flow of the universe. Rhythm puts us in touch with intricacies, inconsistencies, and unpredictable patterns that can awaken us.

Synergetic Awareness

Resonant somatic writing arises from a coherence of mind with flesh, thought with motion, being with becoming, a complexity welcoming feeds from a multiplicity of sources. Awareness is situated in the present moment as it unfolds. The expressiveness of our flesh is not easily reducible to a singular statement or movement, but responsive and reflective of a rich tapestry. Even a simple statement like "I am" can warrant a tome of explication.

The sum achieved through somatic writing is not equal to its parts but greater, creating an integrated and synergetic whole. The coherent awareness, or synergy, is akin to hitting a target while simultaneously taking into account the larger picture. Synergy recognizes how borders spill into and enhance each other. Creativity, knowing, inspiration, and embodiment enhance and expand. Here's where ideas feel paradoxical and challenge balance, like trying to hold water in our hands while walking without losing a drop. Both central and peripheral, we focus on placing words on the line, aligning with a point of view, our narrative, while also accessing currents of inspiration and creativity and allowing their surge.

This is writing from the body, with the body, of the body. Writing is framed as movement, awareness, and expression of our personal existence. We write to be. We write to form being. We write as being. Writing taps into our individual vitality. Our presence is a dance of words. Our being comes across in words as a fragment, an extended passage, a question, exclamation, phrase, comma, and dash. We transcribe ourselves and splash our essence into verbal form. Wave after flesh-born wave crashes upon the shore of the page.

Your body. Your body in motion. Your body stilling itself. Your body in process of articulating itself, reforming and redefining. Your body expressing its aliveness.

Words crossing the page stir the blood, heart, and hormones. Ears vibrate with sound and meaning. Images reflect upon the mind and cells. Rhythm influences phrasing while phrases influence our body, a continuous loop. When we allow the process. When we apply somatic awareness to inform expression, when we embrace momentum and allow our expression to manifest. The approach reveals the relationship between word and body, the word made flesh and the flesh made words.

For Gail who writes fiction, she astonished herself after a period of movement by writing a poem. She says, "I followed what was stirring me when I moved. A sensation caught my interest. I studied it the way you stare at a beautiful damselfly that lands on your arm or a fallen branch in the river. I got down on the floor to better investigate my sensation, to feel. When I sat down to write after, that's when the magic happened." The poem also informed a scene she was working on in a book in process.

We recall ourselves. We write impressions. The impressions form and inform us. We move with all of them. The writing opens us to ourselves. The opening furthers who we are. Writing and then movement or movement and then writing deepens expression, a powerful practice of embodiment. Words happen. Movement happens. Expression happens. Emotion happens. Attention happens. We connect to sensation and to words in the body and on the page. The life pulse, always present, asserts itself with biological delight. Our depths rise up. (*Exercise 4:4: Rhythmic Patterns in Writing*)

Somatic writing is a process of witnessing and expressing the coalescence of the inner and outer worlds and articulating them as an embodied, vitalized, and sustainable verbal knowing. This creative expression enlivens how we dwell in our body, how we show up, feel presence and present ourselves on the line. The words carry weight, energy, and awareness rooted in the listening, moving body. The words carry our knowing and unknowing, furthering understanding, our being in the process of becoming.

The resistance of pen or pencil against paper leaving a trail of ink or lead across the page is a sensual experience, the tapping at the computer more mechanical and repetitive. In writing by hand, the sensory motor skills required to form letters lubricates the writing muscle. We are forced to go slowly, our fingers wrapping around the instrument of expression making micro-movements while ideas link to words. Like a painter brushing colors on a canvas, there's an intimate and artful connection to each letter and word forming. Researchers suggest that writing longhand enhances memory, creativity, and overall learning. They fear losses in brain development among young students whose teachers promote computer use over paper notebooks and pen.[8] Writers such as Joyce Carol Oates and Susan Sontag begin writing by hand and switch to typing once a writing momentum is established. The best method, however, is the one that encourages a writing flow. The best method is what works best for us. Experimenting with writing by hand and typing will determine the difference for ourselves.

Writing About the Body versus Writing from the Body

There are two essential approaches to somatically resonant writing, writing *about* the body and writing *from* the body. The preposition, the "about" and "from," signify a specific relationship between words and the body. The "about" divides and distances the subject (us) from the object (our body) whereas the "from" truncates the distance. The shifting distance is significant. The difference between them raises the question, Who is the I that is writing and how is this I separate from the body that is writing or moving? As a construct, the separation can be helpful.

A traditional first person approach gets us writing about the body as "mine," "my" body, "my" hand or foot or any other part. The "my" implies ownership and suggests some part of us is in control, at least in possession. We look after this possession to the best of our ability. The my perspective contributes to distance because it separate the "me" who is writing from a me that is a body. The me and my lends itself to a relationship in which our body becomes an object to be written about. The separation raises all sorts of philosophical questions once we delve into the identity of the subject and

Writing about or from the body: Celina Alvarez

object and what contributes to these definitions. Aside from owning or possessing our body, what other sort of relationship is possible? Who is this I?

In writing about the body, we might adopt second or third person, a You, He, She, It, and They which further promotes an outsider's perspective. This perspective, or point of view, contributes to the omniscient narrator sometimes used in fiction, a persona that pretends to be an Us with privileged access to the thoughts, memories, and emotions of its characters. This perspective similarly displaces us from our personal body. This works well to a degree in that the body can be considered with greater objectivity and less emotional identification. The dis-identifying loosens the reigns on what is said. We need not fear what is disclosed. We are, after all, not divulging private material about ourselves, merely sharing the thoughts and feelings of a persona with whom we may or may not share common details. The separation encourages the imagination, not bound by usual constraints, to fill in gaps. We can use literary conventions in combination with imagination to explore ourselves. Writing with imagination can convey the complexity of language and expression and bypass limitations and simplifications of literal truth. We get to say what we dared not otherwise. We get to raise dark matter from our depths to the surface.

Or not. We may not know what writing reveals until we open to a narrative stream culled from the rivers of energy flowing through us.

Writing about the body is a powerful activity. We may write about the "me" of the body or write about the elbow or esophagus. We may highlight a specific part of ourselves and come to know that part better. We come to learn its shape, function, sensations, utterances, and stories. We learn about its history, restrictions, and the path to greater flexibility. Writing about a specific part of our body may be the very activity that situates us as students excelling in listening to our somatic self. The focus is expansive and life affirming. The focus deepens an embodied relationship. *(Exercise 4:5 Writing About the Body)*

When we write *from* the body, the distance and separation between word and body shrinks. The visceral immediacy increases. The writing more closely aligns with being in a way we may not have previously experienced. The narrator or I of the writing may be our foot, blood, or any other part of ourselves, and we as holders of the pen or keyboard are its translators. This approach to writing requires an imaginative leap, but it effectively bypasses usual cognitive methods that may stymy getting to the heart and energy of our matter.

I have witnessed numerous breakthroughs in my students and clients who employ this technique. "I didn't know my ankle had so much to say," said Maya after her ankle, injured during dance practice, ranted about its abuse, information that led to investigating her posture. The body, or any part, speaks its mind. This literary construct leads to expressive possibilities for fleshing out bodily events and tapping into embodied wisdom. This approach also deepens an embodied relationship. *(Exercise 4: 6 Writing From a Part of the Body)*

With this approach the writing is the event itself and does not need to reflect on a past or future event. The writing is presence incarnate unfolding itself moment by moment. Abilities, attentions, distractions, feelings, and thoughts all distill into words. The writing propels itself without concern for content and is a stream of words and phrases similar to the free writing promoted by Dorothea Brande, author of *Becoming a Writer*, and Peter Elbow in *Writing Without Teachers*. However, what distinguishes somatic writing from general free writing is the awareness of the body. Prior to or concurrent to the writing, we have established an awareness of the body that now influences the raw verbal stream. We don't stand on the shore and dip toes into the water. We are the current. The body is not writing *about* experience but *is* experience. The process generates experience rather than using language to distill or analyze experience. Each phrase extends our body into a coalescence on the line intersecting interior and exterior worlds.

The "about" and "from" approaches to somatic writing both elucidate the body as an expressive process that supports embodiment. Writing is recognized as a function of the body. The activity of our body lives on the verbal plane. The writing is not apart from the body any more than a yawn. Words assemble on the line to tell a story, express a poem or song, to sound breath and meaning, to contain the uncontainable, and to transmit being.

Writing becomes a way to hear our body's whispers, to stretch thought, to shine a light into an unlit room. It's a way to acknowledge, voice, visualize, and reform energy. The writing reveals our body's knowing as it rides and embodies its currents. The writing can disrupt our usual habits and perceptions and awaken a more inclusive, embodied experience of self whose limits surpass the common reach of our skin.

We tell. We say. We open. Our elbow shares how it got broken. Our lungs share what takes its breath away. The shoulders rant about burdens. The writing shares what moves us and what has taken up residency in our body. We hear ourselves. We attend to our voices, visions, and verbal expression. We listen. Deeply.

The content and discontent of our writing lives in our flesh. Writing arises from the ether of our mind, from sensation in our gut or back, from a thought, a hunch, a fleeting impression. It emerges from the stretch and reach of our connective tissue, from the shortness of our breath, the ache in our knee, from the migraine, our slouch, the way we purse our lips, and how moving the arm or torso or toe is welcomed or resisted. Our writing arises from the marks and motions life imprints upon us, the ones we know and the ones kept close to the bone hidden from easy access.

The writing affects us. A narrative forms and is revised, meaning emerges and is honed, a storyline takes shape, a poem is inspired, our body engaging in a reflexive relationship with words. We may deem a narrative too limiting or a previous perceived truth holds less sway. We release emotion and tension and adopt a new perspective. A poem dawns from a stretch in our trapezius muscle, from turmoil in the gut or a walk in the woods. Interested in the impact of writing on trauma, psychologist James Pennebaker conducted a study in which participants spent fifteen minutes writing expressively over four consecutive days. His findings revealed participants experienced improved immune system function, less stress, lower blood pressure, and increased positive short and long term mood changes.[9]

Trauma, joy, sadness, curiosity, awe, are all sufficient motivations to write and articulate the processes of our body. In expressing ourselves on the line, we are invited to create in the present and actively engage ourselves. The focus is renewing. We see possibilities. We become possibilities. Breath and step, word and phrase, heat and how, all meet and are up for grabs in how we choose to express them. Here lies a moment of liberation. Here we shift our relationship to what has already taken place with what is taking place. We live on the line. We verbalize life. We live in motion. We move life. Our bones and cells and breath and life pulse guide the course.

Moving into Writing and Writing into Movement

At the core of somatic writing is a meeting and collaboration of writing and movement, using one to further the awareness and articulation of the other. It doesn't matter which comes first. Somatic awareness accompanies both. The process of writing includes a deep listening to the body. The process of movement includes a deep listening to language.

We are not doing both simultaneously, one hand strategically typing away, the other cavorting a wave, but as part of the same process. The process may initially be challenging. An appeal of movement is that it is prelingual. Movement happens. It is concrete and fleshy, not conceptual and abstract. Our arm lifts. We turn our head. Our temperature rises. We bleed. Neurons fire. There's no need while moving to analyze nor assign language to the activity. Instead we connect with the sensuality of motion, perhaps how the neck twist relaxes the shoulders and the breath deepens. In surrendering to motion, giving in to the body's natural inclinations, our perceptions heighten. We pay attention, not because an outside source commands we do so, but because the activity itself is captivating. We engage motion with a childlike curiosity, an inventor's inquisitiveness, or the whim of an enthusiast. There is no critical judgement, only sensory connection to our body.

Consequent to motion follows writing. We may write about any part of what took place while moving, how the twisting neck difficult since a soccer injury now makes way for increased flexibility that is frightening but also exhilarating. Or we write about or from the subtle energy roused while we moved.

We let the body lead us to words, let it be our guide, teacher, goad, and muse. Because we have been moving with somatic awareness and listening attentively, the quality and content of our writing is likely to change. Combinations of words habitually chosen no longer suffice. New phrases, voice, rhythm, image, and energy show up. The line takes us where we may not have gone before. We may find every syllable matters, that we repeat words to repeat words because repeating words loosens tightness at our belly. Or we abandon commas altogether and revolt against all punctuation and syntax and propriety because we want to finally do our thing yes finally because in every other area of our life we are fulfilling obligations and thankless visions not ours and now it's our time and we've waited too long. We connect to the sensuality of writing and voicing the body. We do so because a bodily relationship to language brings us home to the earth, to the flesh of our body, and to the heart of being and purpose.

After writing, we may want to follow up with movement. The movement furthers the expressive flow already taking place. A few questions to consider are:

- How can we put any of our words into motion and embody them consciously?
- Do our words arise from a region of the body or from multiple regions?
- How can we move with sound, meaning, emotion, image, or anything else associated with our words?
- What is the somatic impact and influence of the words?

We may consider a literal meaning but equally or more important is the figurative meaning, any image, metaphor, dream, or vision that gets stirred. We listen deeply with whatever sense activates. Suppose you came up with "spinning like a top" while writing. To pair the image with motion in your body, you may twirl your entire body, your spine in axis with the floor. Or you use only your wrist and explore twisting and wobbling. You directly, concretely, and corporeally come to know the words. You can do the same with an exclamation like "Oh, wow!" The two beats may conjure striking motion which can be done by jutting out the chin or reaching quickly with both arms. Explore the meanings in your body until they make sense to you. Understanding arises from their felt presence in our body. Or don't move at all, but imagine yourself moving and welcome the subtle motion taking place. (*Exercise 4:7 Moving the Written Phrase*)

Whether we start with writing or start with moving is unimportant. What takes place is one furthering the exploration and articulation of the other. We move into writing. We write into motion. They launch each other. The result is a greater felt sense, a depth of connection and clarity in what we are doing or have done. It's the difference between feeling okay and feeling pressure at the right ventricle and tingles along the spine. It's the difference between borrowing a word from the dictionary to place on a chair and tailoring it to fit our hips or our chest or our breath. We find what matters most in our body, what is core and what is distal, where the flow slows and where it surges. We find tendencies in our tendons and meaning in our bones. We find how we arrive one foot after another into the direction and balance of our life.

A Somatic Journey

Framing our exploration in words and movement as a somatic journey gets us to recognize the shape of an experience. It shifts casual attention into a deeper probe. We are prepared for rearranging the ordinary into the extraordinary, a hidden perception coming to the foreground.

Toni took two workshops with me. In the first one she composed a beautifully crafted fairy tale, her fiction voice rising up with bold imaginative strength. The vividness and emotional power of it surprised her as did the fact that it flowed easily. She didn't outline or employ common plotting strategies. The second workshop surprised her as well. While doing a body scan and deeply listening, she uncovered an ache in her back that led to a new meaning about a memory. The recovery of information informed her about a recent divorce and relieved her pain. With her permission, I include Toni's writing in its entirety below without changing words or punctuation:

> I set an intention: "to connect deeply with the energy of ME; to get grounded and move into wholeness." I wrote it down, and then it was time to move into my body. I laid down

on the floor with as much of me touching ground as possible. In scanning my body, looking for a place that needed attention, I found the dark curve of my lower back. With my eyes closed, I saw the words "let go" floating under the curve, between the curve and the floor.

I began to free write, letting the words come. "seeing the dark space of my lower back— the curve, the curve over the floor, the arch, like a bridge, like a train trestle, like the aqueducts..." I started drawing the arch as I was envisioning it. (I attached an image that is similar to what I was drawing.) I wrote "the forces that hold up the arch are many, not one. The force pushes both ways to balance—holds in tension. Pull out one stone it would all fall." Then, a little further on: "my dark place. Tension. Let go."

A memory was swirling around, through the writing. I remembered when I was 22, getting married, and my lower back "went out" the day before the wedding. My muscles were twisted and knotted, the pain was unbearable. It threw my back out of alignment. The morning of the wedding, I was stuck in a leaning-over position. I decided to just straighten up in one swift move. I fainted and woke up on the floor. I insisted on going on with the wedding and a sports doctor manipulated my back until it was straight, but I couldn't move it. The pain was incredible. HE commented that all my muscles in my back were so tense that it was like rubber bands pulled too tight—they snapped back into a snarl. I have reflected on all that back pain and the connection to being tense. It wasn't just tension. It was fear and dread that my mind wouldn't allow itself to face. My mother-in-law was frightening. My husband-to-be wasn't defending me. I believe my body knew what the mind wouldn't admit—that there was abuse woven into those relationships, that I had experienced abuse from both of them. I was heading into danger.

I have considered the arch of my back "a weak spot." But now I was envisioning it as a strong arch. I saw darkness under it, and I saw it was holding me up, if I would let go of the tension. And if I would appreciate it! IF I would listen to it. I lived with the pain off and on for years. I had only resolved it with chiropractics and massage that would straighten me out when tension set in to pull me out of alignment. But lying on Cheryl's floor, many pieces of my pain in that 25 year marriage came together. I saw how my backbone held my body up so air could get in and fill it up. I wrote about my memories of my early marriage, of how he humiliated me when I sang him a love song, telling me I didn't sing well. I didn't sing for a long time after that. Even when I did, I felt I didn't have enough air, couldn't take enough in. In the last year of the marriage the feeling of being out of breath was constant.

I saw in my mind how the bridge of my back was strength, how it held me up and gave me space for air. I heard my body telling me what I need to do—to trust it. To let go.

Toni's listening and consequent letting go shows how the body is its own GPS system. At all times, it knows where it is, the conditions of the present, and the direction to course correct. It broadcasts its needs and inclinations. It lets us know through sensation. But as often happens, some part of us gets in the way.

Connecting somatically with words tied to the body is an opportunity to get out of our way. We listen to the body conveying its messages. We open the ear of our heart, our gut, our motion.

Connecting somatically with words gets us to say yes to what we may have said no to out of habit, because somewhere along the way to adulthood, we've been told to trust the mind over the body. The process opens us to the force pulsing through our limbs and our utterances. The process gets us to live inside our words and our words to flesh out what the body senses, what it knows kinetically and proprioceptively. It's up to us to be responsive to the life pulse, to find our body in language and the language in our body.

Writing Approach: Word Flow

Mihaly Csikszentmihaly popularized the phenomenon of flow in his book of the same name where he describes an experience of optimal fulfillment and engagement that is achievable among individuals across a range of disciplines, from executives to athletes to artists. The state in which people are so involved in an activity that nothing else seems to matter. He says, "[T]he experience itself is so enjoyable that people will do it even at great cost, for the sheer sake of doing it."[10] In flow we completely immerse in an activity. Word after word, phrase after phrase rises up from the body, with the body and settles on the page. Little else deters us while we write. Everything about writing consumes our attention. Every mark on the page is like a flock of swans approaching the dock where we dangle our feet in the water. We can't help but notice the float of the feathered swimmers and the faint wake of their glide.

Phrase after phrase emerges like a slow, welcome coil of smoke or an intense flicker of flames that reminds us that every word matters and can be the difference between feeling warmed and getting burned. Every word and every phrase honors the beat of heart, the pulse of blood, us grounding ourselves in the present moment as it unfolds on the line with and without mistakes, with and without concise and elegant phrasing, without and without associated memories, questions, and observations.

We may or may not understand the ramifications of what we're doing. Only write. Only drip or trickle or gush or rant or breathe onto the page. Focus is concentrated, a balance of tension and ease, inspiration and containment, our sole concern to continue. In writing, no thought pulls the hand away from its mission on the page. Images, ideas, sounds, syntax, grammar all find home on the page which spurs the writing onward just as in movement, no thought pulls us away from our gestures, the pattern or chaos of every crimp, bend or stretch engaging us further in the momentum.

We are watchful but do not interfere. We direct but do not control. We recognize the life pulse as fully activated and ride its currents. We yield. We allow the emergence of primal energy.

Flow feels trance-like, as if a force larger than us guides our actions, a second hand other than ours is steering the verbal wheel of our body. We don't relinquish our hold on the wheel, not altogether. We have as formidable a say in the direction and outcome as this second hand yet with its assistance, a universal force compels our writing and moving, resetting any distractions as purposeful and essential. As if awaiting their turn, phrases in writing and movement come forward and settle into position. Language and movement burst through silence and stillness to announce their birth awakening us to their animating power. Stopping violates the natural current whose sole aim is to abide the laws of nature. Our role is to transfer the impulses of our body into a verbal and movement stream. Onward! Onword!

The Perfection of this Moment

Every step along the way is perfect.

Ha, you say, maybe for those with a great life and a gift for writing, but certainly not for me.

For everyone. Each step is essential to the process. There is not a right and wrong step. There is only this step, the one we're currently taking. There is only whatever writing and movement comes forth. There is only this breath, this observation, this sensation. Track them. Welcome them. Every step which gives the initial appearance as good or bad, on point or graceless, full of beauty or blather, contains a gift. Greet them all with curiosity. What is defined initially as a mistake is not an error but the very material in the process of becoming. Each step contributes to unfolding expression and to finding out what's possible, what wants to emerge. Each step honors What Is. We are not in struggle, but moving with the energy that presents itself. We allow. In allowance, energy moves freely and is not blocked.

Where does each step lead? To knowing what we feel and think and unraveling our shortsightedness for a broader vision. To jumping into the puddle of our life. To seeing what the quiet and raucous focus of our attention reveals. To perceiving the flesh that matters. To honoring each and every breath, the twist of our tongue, and how a word falls flat and then lifts its head. To hearing what the body is saying. To honoring this saying as one welcomes the rain, snow, shine, and cool.

Exercises

Exercise 4:1 Defining Writing

- For what purposes have you used writing? Come up with a new way that aligns with your body and your needs. Jot down ideas without concern for how to manifest them.

Exercise 4:2 Resonance

- Choose a word from the list below and close your eyes. Using deep listening and inner vision, notice where in your body the word resonates. You may experience it as a sensation, an image, a hunch, or something else. Use your imagination if needed.

Impoverish	Democracy	Health
Succulent	Trigger	Nomad
Feisty	Cornered	Festive

- Once you locate where the word resonates, sense the space in the area. What does it look and feel like? For instance, is it dark, rubbery, numb, hot?
- How is the word written? For instance, is it bold, italicized, blue neon, Helvetica? How does its lettering impact you?
- Write about the relationship between the word and its region. Write freely. Use imagination.
- *Variation*: Use words of your own.

Exercise 4:3 Pacing

This exercise helps determine what writing speed supports somatic awareness. You will be switching attention back and forth between writing and its somatic resonance. As you write, notice where in your body you feel a reverberation or any other sensation. Your attention may not be consistently on the line or your body, but do your best to keep awareness of both. Any writing topic can be used, however, let's go with How Your Body Writes.

- Fast: Write quickly whatever words come forth. Don't be concerned with correctness or judgements. Keep the words coming. At several junctures as is possible, turn attention to your body. Where do you feel the words resonate? What is their location? What else do you notice?
- Slow: Continue writing whatever words come forth, but do so slowly. Go slow enough to pause your attention and locate the word's reverberation in your body. Pause as needed to feel resonance before resuming writing. You may want to stop at a noun, verb, image, or punctuation. What do you notice?
- Between: Vary your speed to the sweet spot that allows a comfortable writing flow balanced with an awareness of bodily resonance. Find the speed that works best. Try a few speeds along the continuum of Fast and Slow.

Exercise 4:4 Rhythmic Patterns in Writing

What follows are several writing prompts. Each prompt contains a rhythm and a blank. Repeatedly write the phrase and fill in the blank. Filling the blank is not a matter of filling in with a correct answer. Consider it a response. Use each prompt for at least a page. While writing, notice what occurs somatically.

- I am my best when I _____ and my worst when I _____.
- I had to say it. The words rushed out. I hadn't thought I'd say it. I opened my mouth. Up they came. Out. I said _____.
- My heart beat. My going. My belly rivaling my pelvis. I sit up. Creature comforts. I resist names. This is my story. It begins with _____. Or doesn't. It being with _____.

Exercise 4:5 Writing About the Body

- Choose any part of the body.
- Tell its story using "my" as in my forehead or my pelvis. The story uses this region as the primary focus. Perhaps it was the time your forehead was the unfortunate recipient of a fishing hook or an understanding about how a specific angle of the pelvis supports walking.
- You might want to include an outsider's perspective of that body part. How does that perspective differ or coincide with yours?

Exercise 4:6 Writing From a Part of the Body

- Choose a part of the body for which you want greater understanding.
- Let that part tell its story. The narrator, or I, is for instance, your hair or skin or heart. Let it share information or tell a tale. Give it personality, attitude, and a voice unlike yours. This writing can be a story, a dialog, an email exchange or another form.
- What does that body part revealed that you didn't know previously?

Exercise 4:7 Moving the Written Phrase

- Choose a phrase from your writing that appeals to you for whatever reason.
- Explore the phrase in movement. Consider its imagery, meaning, and the sound of each letter and syllable. Come up with a movement that corresponds literally or figuratively with the phrase.
- Repeat the movement and vary it. Relocate the motion. For instance, if you were shaking a leg, you might shake an arm. Consider making it larger, smaller, slower, or faster.
- Let the motion become another motion either deliberately or through

happenstance. Let the motion take you on a movement journey. Notice sensation, images, memories, and feelings.
- Write *about* the movement journey. What took place?
- *Variation*: Write *from* the body, continuing a quality of the movement in writing. For instance, if your motion was shaking, write with a shaky sensibility.

5

The Imagining Body

Sylvia rose from her chair, rooted her feet to the floor and brought her arms parallel, then lowered toward her waist. Just prior, I had instructed the group to use their imagination to come up with a visual symbol and corresponding movement, a kinesthetic representation for a current writing project. Repeatedly she opened and closed her arms like a bellows. As she fanned something invisible, her motion got mechanical, her entire body more rigid. When I reminded her to notice any messages from her body, any inklings of a want, the fanning motion softened and she twisted her arms to angle the wrists outward. Her posture changed, too, her legs energetically aligning with her arms, her entire body working together, no part struggling against another. She then sat down to write and later shared her experience with the group.

Sylvia explained that she selected a fire with a bellows to fan the heat of her writing project. When she listened more deeply to messages from her body, she realized the motion didn't feel right and angled her wrists outward which felt somehow more appropriate. Through writing, she realized how the initial movement protected her torso and closed herself off to other's influence. Once she angled her arms and wrists outward, she felt more open physically and emotionally. She realized, too, how she'd been closed to hearing feedback on her project, comments that were essential to the realization of her goal.

The Nudge of Imagination

Imagination often gets a bad rap. Misunderstood and underappreciated, it's considered make-believe, fantasy, unreality, child's play, best left behind in childhood. Imagination does not receive the same accolades as reason, logic, and facts which are often considered hallmarks of intelligence. Distaste for imagination is so strong that some children are short changed on developing this ability. Grade school classes that foster imagination frequently have been cut in favor of fact-based Standard of Learning, or SOL, subjects like science and math. Its scarcity contributes to a generation suffering from a poverty of imagination which harms the inventiveness and prosperity of a society. Without imagination, we remain stuck in a limited paradigm, our arms and mind closed to a broader view.

We are enamored by facts. They are the bricks and mortar for fields like law, science, and the development of new technology. Facts help build tunnels beneath a river, ensure a train runs on time, and perform open heart surgery. Facts are essential to understanding how something works and lay a foundation to progress in any number of fields. Facts are evidence. They offer stability and reliability. They present the world as knowable and predictable. Undoubtedly facts are a salve to ignorance.

Imagination is, however, equally important. Imagination helps us envision the possibility of a tunnel, rail road, and open heart surgery. Imagination leads to the blueprints and prototypes for new technology. Imagination is how dancers birth choreography, how writers compose a book, how physicists develop quantum mechanics, how cell biologists discover epigenetics. Martin Cooper with Motorola credits the communicator in the television show *Star Trek* as the inspiration for him creating the first mobile phone. Reading comprehension, too, relies on imagination since understanding words as repre-

Shadow play

sentative of reality requires abstract thinking. Without imagination, there is no creativity, no bold thinking, no broadening horizons, no prodding facts for any flaws or errors. We are sentenced to repetition, to grasping ever more desperately to holding an idea whose usefulness may have expired. Psychologist Marion Woodman goes even further, recognizing that using imagination bolsters the life pulse and could be the difference between life and death. She wrote the following while struggling with and eventually healing from ovarian cancer: "Kill the imagination and you kill the soul. Kill the soul and you're left with a listless, apathetic creature who can become hopeless or brutal or both…. The image magnetizes the movement of the energy."[1]

Imagination hints at the future. It provides a foreshadowing, a whisper, a nudge. It lays down a map of a region we may have not known existed and urges an exploration of a new direction. "Imagination," says Albert Einstein "is everything. It is the preview of life's coming attractions."[2] Imagination carries us where facts reluctantly go. Imagination breaks through dogmatic barriers and habitual blinders and offers alternatives that contain vital insight and improvements. It provides the energy of momentum and gets us to open our eyes, to look and move anew. Today's imaginings spark writing and movement, the light of insight and the life affirming energy propelling us forward. Today's imaginings fuel tomorrow's reality.

Dualism's Short Breadth

Dualism, a theory that recognizes reality as comprised of two irreducible opposing elements, too often contributes to black and white thinking and leads us to believe erroneously that facts and imagination cannot coexist. Whichever side of the divide we stand on, we eye the other side with suspicion, our ego and world view at risk. We stand tight fisted and resolute in our perspective and claim to the right answers. We see no truth or benefit in an opposing view point. Neither curiosity nor the possibility of an unforseen gain compels a peek. An all or nothing mentality renders us inflexible in body and mind, unable to adapt to inevitable changes, be it a broken bone or heart. Our absolutist, self-willed blindness provides false security. I again quote Einstein who mastered situating facts in coexistence with imagination. He says, "If at first the idea is not absurd, then there is no hope for it…. Condemnation without investigation is the height of ignorance."[3]

Dualism stymies finding solutions to formidable problems. It can entrench divisiveness rather than cooperation and constructs walls rather than bridges. It pits one person or group or idea against another and disdains the value of compromise, collaboration, and unity. It rigidifies ideas and, by extension, bodies. It pushes cultivating innovation and sustainable solutions which rely upon establishing commonality, compatibility, and new information into the realm of the impossible.

Dualism simplifies life into manageable categories which is helpful in making decisions—to a degree. But if seen to accurately represent What Is, dualism is harmful in its disregard for huge swaths of experience that don't fit easily into the binaries of an either/or category. Life cannot be distilled into a This Or That perspective. Life is much more diverse and complex. It is full of mystery, paradox, ripe with experiences that defy easy understanding and categorization, every moment bursting with originality and dynamic change. A muscular stretch, for instance, shows there is no simple on/off, flexible/tight dichotomy. Flexibility and strengthening come incrementally, riding on the back of every breath and every contraction and release of a muscle.

It is a malady of being if we fail to recognize complexity. Between black and white thinking lies a vast multi-hued, multi-dimensional area. It is the region where synesthesia hatches, where atoms collide, where joy overlaps with sorrow, where subtle energies rise up the central axis of the body, where This, That, and Another live in close proximity. Nuance and details abound everywhere. They await the deep listening of our eyes and ears and touch and motion. The twist of our wrists and arms, seemingly inconsequential initially, may be the juncture determining whether our project succeeds or never rises up from the flatness of the page.

Feeding our curiosity saves us from the famine of disinterest and fortifies us to withstand daily pressures. Instead the body metabolizes its encounters to bolster healthy cells and place a lift in our stance and expression, to roll with circumstances and speak the language that speaks us into embodiment. The capacity to embrace curiosity and complexity is to embrace the very substance that awakens the bodymind. (*Exercise 5:1 Inviting Imagination*)

We yearn to fit into existence, experience belonging, ease, and self-assuredness. These powerful motivations can make us susceptible to accepting deficient and hastily constructed conclusions. We may stop learning and asking questions. We may hold tight to an antiquated idea whose usefulness has expired. There may be a physical correspondence; we may hold our breath and restrict our diaphragm. We are likely cutting off the flow and influence of the life pulse and ignoring small and repercussion changes taking place everywhere. Our intentions may be good, but leaving out a substantial section of the equation does us a disservice. We repeat actions that lead to dead ends. We stand without grounding our energy or supporting our emotional or psychophysical alignment. We hold opposing views hostage. We may justify our behavior, but in the end discover we have fooled ourselves and robbed the night of its dreams and the day of its inspirations.

After the first class of the semester, Karl told me he would be unable to dance with the girls in our class. Conservatively raised, he believed that girls were weak and not to be touched. I explained that class required all students to partner with each other regardless of gender, touch would be common, and if this was problematic, he should consider attending a different class. Surprisingly, he continued attending and by the end of the semester, his mind having opened, he said, "I didn't know girls could be so strong!"

If we favor imagination while abandoning facts, we support delusion and faulty thinking. We dig a hole for the tunnel yet act surprised when water pours in through the inadequately sealed windows with the panoramic view of the ocean life. The image we move with has, at best, a tenuous correspondence with reality. We unground and go through the motion without feeling connected. We jump from a height without considering the impact on our joints or the mechanics of balance. Perhaps our writing rambles endlessly without touching the core of our being and we hold onto a story or idea with a life pulse denying stubbornness.

An overzealous hold on imagination devoid of facts destroys the chance for ideas to manifest. Our pollyannaish ideation disconnected from facts, experience, and evidence impedes connecting with our body or any body of wisdom. We may feel comforted by our imagination in the short term, but it ultimately cheats of us our breath, well-being, and the fruition of aspirations.

Similarly when we favor facts over imagination, we make few if any substantive steps forward. The world is viewed as static and unchanging. We may clench our jaw and stiffen our neck. An exclusionary and steadfast hold upon facts may provide a sense of security but can be as delusional as relying solely on imagination. We refuse to consider as did scientists in the mid 1800's that washing hands did indeed save lives of patients undergoing surgery, an idea proposed by Ignaz Semmelweiss whose suggestion was mocked and ignored. An exclusive reliance on facts fails to recognize the world and our understanding as dynamic and changing.

Facts hold great appeal in that they give the illusion of certainty. Imagination, too, holds appeal in its portrayal of a preferred and idealized world. Both perspectives are valuable and necessary. Accepting one while rejecting the other renders any understanding flimsy and incomplete, akin to understanding the body without considering the role of the mind or defining a fish without considering the importance of water. Imagination and facts work hand in hand. In coexistence, the difference between truth and falsehood, comprehension and misunderstanding, insight and vision over fear and grasping can be teased out. Reductive thinking is helpful but in combination with creative, evolutive thinking.

Combination is key. Embodiment relies on the coaction of facts and imagination. Facts inform us about the activity of cells, how calcium grows bones, what foods support hormonal and chemical balance and which bodily secretions are signs of health or symptoms of disease. Facts help us measure how breath rhythm changes oxygen levels and brain function. Imagination gets us to listen to and hear our cells—or any other part of our body—and to tie emotional and sensory experience to an idea. Imagination helps us recognize a glimpse or twinge or another fleeting sensation as a clue to insight and the emergence of new life. Imagination acknowledges, even applauds whims and hunches as signposts along the route to development. Imagination provides an entry into our body and illuminates the crevices and ridges of our interior landscape. Imagination holds the path and promise of embodied wisdom.

Among its strengths, imagination bypasses logic and common ways of knowing and works as a portal to perceiving phenomena that ordinary sensing cannot reach. Imagination manifests on its own terms in its own language. It does not always play by familiar rules nor rely on linear thinking. No A to B to C for this friend. Rather it triumphs with leaps in logic. It welcomes impulsiveness and whimsy, mischief and transcendence. It encourages teasing out hunches for their links to truth and vision. It asks us to trust process without knowing the destination. For these reasons, mishaps and missteps in writing and motion, what is typically erased, halted, removed, and shuttled out of the room, needs to be recognized as the imagination breaking through. See it as raw, undeveloped, and emerging material that when given free reign ushers in insights, creativity, and healing. See it as the fledgling prior to flight. Coax it from its nest.

Imagination welcomes a lazy stroll or brisk frolic in all regions of the bodymind and draws upon intuition and the dreamlike unconscious. Imagination relishes in its ability to dart, pounce, and mingle, to make associations between seemingly unrelated material. Imagination doesn't want to be anchored to a specific conception, but have the liberty to float on breath or bone, one foot dangling in string theory while a hand swirls in the foam of a synaesthetic whirlpool. "Your brain," says Emily Dickinson, "is wider than the sky."[4] Your movement and your phrases, I add, can traverse the globe.

Gifts of the Unconscious

The unconscious receives a bad rap. It too readily is understood as a complete absence of awareness, an anesthetized void, a mindless zone missing thought, sensation, daydreams and hope. Consciousness is associated with mindfulness. A cursory understanding of mindfulness however, popularized by meditation in recent decades, can lead to the mistaken conclusion that operating from the unconscious is problematic and that consciousness is paramount. Mindlessness is problematic if we lock into an idea or a constant replay of the past or fantasy about the future. Optimal functioning requires rooting in the sensations, emotions, and awareness of the present. Optimal functioning requires awareness of this moment and this body in collusion with the life pulse, some energies known and some arriving from a distant source.

Undoubtedly consciousness is vital. It helps us exert control over decisions and behaviors. It provides focus and direction. But the unconscious is equally important. To turn away from it is to turn a blind eye to 95 percent of who we are, the figure neuroscientists cite as how much gray area of the brain is devoted to the unconscious.

At all times of day during all activities, the unconscious exerts its influence. It fuels and flavors what we do and how we do it, how we sit and talk, fidget in stillness or write "sty" when we meant to write "sky." It is the storehouse for every event and impression, packed into the connective tissue and

Integrating the shadow: Cheryl Pallant, left, Amy Impellizzeri

cells of our being. Some of what it stores is best left untouched, working in our behalf without it ever rising into awareness. The unconscious operates largely behind the scenes like a director who never steps onto the stage but leaves evidence of influence everywhere, from the placement of a prop to the delivery of dialogue.

If we turn away from the unconscious, we assuredly push a horde of material into our blind spot. Carl Jung refers to the rejected parts of us as shadow. The shadow is the material we refuse to accept and identify as us. The shadow may be unfavorable qualities such as envy, anger, and lust but it may also be favorable qualities such as success and happiness that we believe we don't deserve. Judged as incompatible to our preferred identify, the story we've subscribed to about us, we deny the presence of the shadow and, by extension, its influence. We not only push it to the back of the closet, we may even go so far as refusing to accept that the closet exists.

The denial is harmful and diminishes the life pulse. We may prefer to avoid what makes us uncomfortable, yet this is the very material that holds the key to embodiment. Look it in the eye. Feel the fleeting sensation. Use this material wisely. The shadow contains the seeds for growth, healing, and creative expression.

By looking away and turning against truth, we diminish our abilities. "Everyone carries a shadow," Jung wrote, "and the less it is embodied in the individual's conscious life, the blacker and denser it is."[5] The shadow, a dark pool of unconscious material, leaves an ample trickle of clues. It leaks out, as all unconscious energy does, and can lead to disjointed thinking, despair, disembodiment, and an argument with reality. For instance, we may unconsciously harbor anger and feel a vague dullness in our abdomen, yet end up projecting that anger upon another, insisting it is they, not us, with this feeling. The result may be that we cannot complete a project or do so joylessly. We disembody. We don't connect with what is taking place within and confuse the source. We don't feel our anger, learn from and transform it. We don't perceive the tilt in our walk and pinched nerve which left unattended could become sciatica. What is in shadow remains a stepchild locked out of the house who grows more and more bitter and vengeful with each unheeded cry.

What gets overlooked in our dismissal of the unconscious are its gifts. Among them, the unconscious is largely responsible for creativity. We may choose consciously to create work, however it is the unconscious which provides much of the momentum, content, and aha moments along the way. As we dance and write—or pursue any other creative pursuit—we draw from the material in the storehouse of the unconscious. There's no need to riffle through and identify all the material. Withdrawals can be imprecise and vague, an image not readily understood blowing to the foreground, a phrase or motion sputtering to the surface. We purposefully choose to move and write but we also let movement move us and let writing inscribe us.

The unconscious is also largely responsible for our healing. The symptoms of our unease are the material that wants greater attention, our body motioning us to investigate closer. The symptoms are the warning lights telling us something is amiss. They point to disowned, pushed aside, neglected, and lost parts of us. The symptoms suggest we have strayed off balance and provide an entry toward integrating anew and reclaiming well-being. (Exercise 5:2 Healing with Imagination)

Intuiting Matter

While generating material, analysis and understanding are best delayed. Engage the conceptual and critical skills later. Creativity prefers a yielding to the flow and surges of energy. Like a dream that evaporates readily once we awake, creativity prefers sticking to its dreamlike momentum. Once the spigot to the unconscious is twisted open, energy streams from deep within the cells, from interstitial fluids, from every crevice of our bodymind.

Making time and space for welcoming the unconscious is a tremendous gift. The unconscious needs a place to emerge and roam. It wants to be felt, seen, expressed, and acknowledged. The body needs the right circumstance to let down its guard, an authentic and open presence to counter years of armoring and hiding. A safe container or structure with specific guidelines makes it possible. It creates a welcome space for raw, unprocessed material to emerge for the expansion and focus of new breath, expression, and understanding. A wild haired vision, the emotional tangle of trauma, absurdity rallying alongside the sensible, a body and mind turned, seen from another angle in the room under the light of a newly installed bulb are all welcome. The container encourages this material to come forth. The process enables us to rebalance who we are, to become more ourselves, to shift the emotional charge, and integrate at a new level. We uncover options previously unavailable because we may have been too busy, enslaved to habits, fear, or safe ideas, and the perpetuation of complacency. Moving the energy of the unconscious honors the somatic body.

The container creates an experience that is free of everyday obligations and routine. For a brief reprieve, a load off our usual feats, we practice a new order, center in spaciousness, allowing a chance to refresh, reboot, and renew. We explore the turning of our wrists. We embody the word "turn" or "twist."

We poke at dictionary meanings. We see which meaning, if any, fits personal experience. We ground in the moment as a physical inquiry and an investigative laboratory for being. We unplug from the usual socket and redirect intention and attention, testing balance and ease, seeking a middle ground between suffering and bliss, giving our body a choice, not a given.

Here lies embodiment at is best. We are tapping into the rapid-fire circuitry of our synaptic dance, nerves emitting, the body on cue and in flow, the energy of the body doing what it does best, cells transporting the intelligence of its DNA, intuiting and pulsing new life. This subtle yet profound rhythm allows our body to harmonize with the flesh of being, through every subcutaneous and biotic channel of expression. We pulse, flow, and intuit.

Intuition is direct knowing, direct experience, information coming to us from somewhere with a blurred return address and no tracking code. Intuition comes from a body engaged in deep listening, intimate with its barely perceptible workings. Dance and movement therapist Linda Hartley suggests intuition arises from sensitivity to the breath of the cells as they expand and contract. She says,

> Intuitive insight, in my understanding, is the result of a complex receiving and processing of information through many channels, which occurs beyond the threshold of conscious awareness; access to cellular wisdom is an important basis for this subliminal process. When we awake cellular awareness and perceive through the cells and the integrated bodymind, we gain access to levels of information which might not be accessible through our external senses in normal states of consciousness.[6]

Key here is stepping out of a normal state of perceiving and consciousness into a heightened state. We feel into the depths. We connect to our body and to the subtle emanations of energy. We sense beyond the usual responsiveness and access the channels that contribute to our becoming.

Among her proposed practices, Hartley recommends visualizing cells, followed up by direct kinesthetic experience, or somatization, a term borrowed from fellow movement therapist Bonnie Bainbridge Cohen. An example of somatization is feeling and knowing what we may have previously believed inaccessible, like awareness of cells. Connecting with the mind and breath of cells is cellular breathing. Cohen says, "Cells resonate in relationship to each other. As more cells within us become aware of themselves and are responsive, there is a fuller resonance between them, and we experience inner balance and self-knowing."[7] *(Exercise 5:3 Cellular Breathing)*

We can know more than we think we know. We can feel with greater intricacy into the hollows of our flesh. Our sensing goes beyond common sensing. Following the body's energy leads us to imagining and manifesting possibility. We go where the body seems to be calling and listen closely.

Reintegrating

The process of writing and moving with somatic awareness brings the unconscious into awareness and shuffles experience and understanding. Remote and hidden material has an opportunity to integrate into conscious to broaden awareness and understanding. Feelings surface and shift. Clues from the wisdom of the body show up. Space opens for new experience grounded in the present moment.

The unconscious feeds the imagination. It is its wellspring. Imagination welcomes multiplicity in singularity, hope within fear, the invisible visible, the unheard heard, the body stepping into itself, transforming phenomenon with a strike of a pen, a gesture, an image rising out from the haze. Synesthesia and paradox abound as opposing elements rub against each. Imagination warns us not to rush to simple conclusions nor translate phenomena literally. Consider Rene Magritte's painting "Ceci n'est pas une pipe" (This is not a pipe) as a reminder, the image of a pipe juxtaposed by a statement refuting the picture. So is it or is it not a pipe? And if it's not a pipe, then what is it? It's unlikely that the imagination will refute a conclusion; rather, it shows elements to be malleable and unfixed. As we engage the multiple streams accessible through somatic awareness, our perceptions change through noticing sensation, emotion, movement, sounds, memories, and images.

Carl struggled with social anxiety. Speaking up within a group and bringing any attention to himself was terrifying. He shared this information in a near whisper, his shoulders rounding inward, his eyes meeting mine briefly before looking away. He chose the image of an eagle as an example of freeing himself from the clutches of his fear. He widened the wings of his arms slowly at first, as if the motion strained his muscles and he couldn't hold his arms aloft. He persisted though, his arms gradually opening further as if soaring, his face flushing from the rush of blood. From his flight and consequent writing, he recalled memories of constant criticism from his father. He wrote about the hurt of his father's words as well as the joy of flying above it all. His heart opened to forgotten pain, to new sensations and a lessening of his anxiety. Using his imagination and motion helped him connect more deeply with his body and access stored away material.

Imagination acknowledges perception and meaning as layered, associative, cause and effect not as linear and certain as may be preferred. In loosening our grasp for absolutes, the body's defenses relax and the bodymind's shutters open. The need for certainty subsides. Our body relaxes into ambiguity, form in process, life unfolding. Our eyes can see into darkened corners, the closet door ajar. We feel more at liberty to bend down to hands and knees and handle our finds with curiosity. The subtleties of proprioception and kinesthetic awareness bring new sensations to the foreground as informative, insightful, resonant, and, at times, crucial in cases concerning our health.

Imagination may take substantive leaps or crawl from one sensation, emotion, and image to the next. A choreographer may hear music as motion. A writer may transform tension in her neck into a story about a woman who lost her family home to fire. Imagination welcomes a motley crew of influences and forges intersections, collisions, overlaps, and parallel pathways. Imagination experiences the bodymind as boundless, all experience connected in obvious and inconspicuous ways. Imagination supports heightened perceptions and presence. It waters the seeds of new vision and embodiment and deep bodily knowing. Imagination knows that paradox and contradiction share much in common despite seeming chasms of differences. Imagination relies on a life pulse whose tributaries cascade openly as well as furtively, an interconnected system not typically perceived with a single, cursory glance.

Pairing kinesthetic and proprioceptive abilities with imagination powers the body to open the doors of perception. Sensations shake us up and wake us up. We cannot ignore a belly flutter or sudden change in temperature. We cannot ignore a swoon that may result in toppling us toward the floor before we regain balance. For most of us, given the sensory dominance of eyes, imagination manifests visually. An image appears in a flash or emerges slowly like the moon from behind clouds. We see an eagle. We see a wingspan crowded by the room. We see the walls of the room collapse. It may make immediate sense—you recognize feathers as freedom from a past event—or it may be random and nonsensical. Making immediate sense is unimportant since pursuing meaning prematurely limits impact. Better to let the image capture attention and let it propel you forward. View the image as if it were a movie or a dream. Watch. Feel how it moves you. Let the image unfold on its own. Witness life energy flowing. Meander with the field of your imagination.

Engage motion with imagination and the body fills in sensory gaps. Movement has a way of convincing us. It renders the dreamlike state of imagination to feel palpable and real, the combination reinforcing neural pathways. Choreographer and researcher Ivan Hagendoorn reports that the motor cortex of the brain is activated whether we imagine motion or actually move, the reason dancers and athletes are encouraged to imagine their activity prior to performance as a way to improve their ability. The brain, it seems, conflates them.[8]

The imagination is the nudge and nod urging further investigation. What may initially come across as random and nonsensical are the very stepping stones of creativity, healing, invention, and integration. They carry an essence or seed. They are the surprise parcels delivered with an undecipherable scribble for a return address. Carry them into your study. Unpack their contents and use them as props. See them as mementoes sent to yourself, as fodder for somatic growth, instruments for your somatic journey. Establish a relationship to them. Write them down. Move with them. Feel their presence, their light and shadow, and how your gut or heart responds. Watch them change shape and color and texture and emotive charge. Give them synesthetic wings that fly you to new insights. (*Exercise 5:4 Words and Motion Arising*)

Frequent practice reinforces getting better at recognizing the contents of our imagination and discerning the difference between common fantasies, such as the boogie man beneath the bed, from genuine glimpses of intuition and somatic wisdom. Common fantasies trap us in a sticky web of disembodiment whereas those more genuinely rooted in the body provide clues that inform and liberate us. Learn to trust our body, to note subtle and obvious differences between one sensation and another. Pay attention to anomalous as well as familiar patterns of motion, emotion, and sensation. Extend the reach. Heed the sinewy dialog that our body uses to speak.

The Power of Symbol and Metaphor

The power of imagination is in the energy it carries. Imagination transports that energy and functions as its outward manifestation, a mask, a place holder, and container. It allows the focus of attention to be placed on a perceptible element such as words or motion. It can function like a dream whose images and actions are not to be taken literally. It brings attention to surface appearances while simultaneously pointing elsewhere and may be the closest we get to experiencing its otherwise vague and elusive essence.

Imagining slows down neuronal activity to alpha waves, about 7.5 to 14 Hertz per second. The slower rhythm stirs a neurochemical brew that opens channels to the subconscious and a dreamlike, meditative awareness. The rhythm takes us places that normal waking consciousness does not. Normal waking consciousness, by contrast, is characterized by beta waves, about 14 to 40 Hertz per second, which supports reason and decision making. Cognitive neuroscientists Christopher Berger and Henrik Ehrsson have concluded that sensory signals generated by imagination change both the quality of perceptions and the senses that do the perceiving.[9] Imagination transforms the imperceptible into the perceivable, the immaterial into the material, and the imagined into the possible.

As tools of the imagination, metaphors and symbols prove to be particularly potent, given that they operate on more than one level simultaneously. Metaphors are substitutes, a comparison between two unlike things, one used to understand the other. For instance, the unfamiliar taste of a frog is frequently compared to the common gustatory experience of eating chicken. Symbols take analogies further. Their inner meaning indicates a deeper or universal truth, pointing out a direction and dispatching us across its relational terrain. Symbols evoke and catalyze the psyche and shift understanding. Their energy carries us beyond our current perception. We step forth with one part of our brain, then illuminate another area. We generate a neurochemical wave reinforced by the next. Imagination functions as a signpost and sometimes the entire map. *(Exercise 5:5 Manifesting with an Embodied Symbol)*

Psychologist Ralph Metzner identifies several archetypal spiritual metaphors with transformative power: the tree of life, the alchemical fire, the veil of illusion, journeying, death and rebirth, awakening, among others. He recognizes their function as "connecting links between states and levels of consciousness, bridging different domains of reality…. The most important function of a symbol is to induce or catalyze changes in our perceptions, feeling, or thinking."[10] The potent metaphors and symbols often connected with elaborate myths are found in various religious traditions and can shift awareness from one paradigm to another. However, if we adopt a metaphor or symbol without checking in with ourselves somatically we may never activate its energy. Choosing a suitable catalyzing metaphor or symbol takes place through sensing and deep listening. The symbol may be used for centuries or one based on a personal somatic inquiry and be as common as breath and as delighting as a fragrant touch of the divine. *(Exercise 5:6 Transformative Image)*

Finding a transformative symbol: Yoa Thompson

5. The Imagining Body

A symbol may be archetypal as is the tree of life or commonplace like a shoe. To determine their potency, symbols are best tested by consulting the body for feedback. If the symbol arises on its own, it is worthy of pursuit. Entertain it for a bit to tease out its helpfulness, if there's to be any. My student Kris kept receiving images of gardens and gardening week after week while moving and writing. Because she disliked gardening, their persistence confused her. I urged her to consider the image and not hastily exile it based on her antipathy. The workshop ended with no insight. A few months later, I ran into Kris who told me that after months of trying, she was pregnant. Gardening was her body's way of informing her of the life growing within.

How did her body know? How could it not? Missing her period was a common occurrence so that didn't cue her. But her blood and hormones knew and tried to convey it through an image she might understand. She only pieced it together when she went to the doctor for an unrelated symptom and took a pregnancy test.

Here I return attention to the bioelectric field that is always present, interacting with the fields of people, animals, plants, rocks, and all manner of objects. This field full of atoms, waves, and particles dances near and beyond easy reach of the five senses. Imagination overrides the limits of ordinary sensing. Imagination is a perceptual filter to the activity in this field. The previously insensible translates into an image (for the visually dominant) or word (for the verbally dominant) or movement (for the kinesthetic dominant). The raw material finds entry into our perceptions, initially appearing imaginative, unreal, and whimsical until its further significance is fleshed out. It's up to us to listen with all our senses with a pliant bodymind to pursue clues on whatever sensory level they are presented. The imagination is the window between worlds. It is up to us to lift our body over the sill.

We may not be expecting guests, yet hear the knock and attend to the door. We give the raw material voice and gesture and image. We dance what we detect, our body assuming its shape, tone, or gesture. We still and watch its forming design like a waft of smoke. We assign words to murmurs. We tell the story of a sensation. We thrust our head out the window to wind and speak in the voice of our cousin or brother who chases foxes and we run in place to know what it means to chase and be chased, to fox and to outfox. Words and images resonate in our body and on the line. We put ourselves on the line to express the previously unexpressed and to see who we have been, who we are, and who we are becoming, the expression essential if we are to grow beyond our current state and honor the process of life. We move from the center and perimeter of our being and quiver with any break in the design. We lift a leg and a hope which flush the heart with blood and the courage to say yes to what needs affirming and no to what needs discarding. We exhale. We pause. We place periods and new paragraphs where we need to separate one moment from the next. We write the truth of this moment. We write about gardening or blood. We lie on the floor and lift a leg to the horizon of our knowing. We twist in place and extend up through the spine. We express ourselves along the continuum of what hides and what manifests, what wants to be seen and what shows us to ourselves. With each step, the weight of our flesh beckons attention.

Actively Imagining from Far Afield

Sometimes particulars from our biofield make their own way into our awareness as a result of chance. Without our inquiry, something appears unexpectedly and out of context and we wisely notice. Other times the imagination must be pursued, coddled and jostled, the stage set, the body warmed, the ink ready to spill across the page. The imagination responds well to intentional and active cultivation and welcomes an invitation. Psychologist Carl Jung referred to this cultivating as active imagination, a technique that transforms contents of the unconscious into images, narratives, and other perceivable phenomenon. Actively imagining accesses states of being that provides an experiential path to knowing. Deliberate imagining assists in revealing and coming to know parts of us otherwise not readily accessible or perceivable. With imagination engaged, what hovers in consciousness shifts into a new location while what hides in the subcutaneous and ethereal hollows of the unconscious slides into view. A heightened and more expansive attentiveness gets us to see, hear, feel, and notice from this alpha wave state.

By actively imagining, we may turn a simple light into a shimmer that enervates our spine. We may turn a shoulder tension into an exquisite undulation. An achy throat may sputter into a guttural poem. Sensing and knowing, wondering and wandering all shuffle into new positions, turning an aversion into a verse, an unsettled question into a strength, a hunch into a revelation. What hadn't been or could be shimmies into What Is. The emphasis is on actively engaging and furthering the initial image, motion, or sensation.

In turning imperceptible phenomena into a focus for engagement, we move with an image that arises from imagination. Or we write about an impromptu image arising from the body such as the garden. We combine writing and moving, embody an image, embody words, the imagining body leading the way, alert to the presence of raw material from the field shifting into our greater awareness.

5. The Imagining Body

The process of actively engaging imagination increases awareness. We engage with fleeting and unfamiliar sensations, feelings, movement, and images, deliberately expanding upon them with curiosity and play. We follow the crumbs dropped on the path, pocket and turn them over with our tongue until they dissolve. We pursue the dream of their logic, watching what characters, voices, gestures or insights emerge to increase our feeling and understanding which honors the life force. We sit up. We edge our ear toward hearing secrets. We lure the shadow into a dance with light. We sense opening the grounded body.

We don't always know how we know. Sometimes, fragments of images, thoughts, feelings and hunches show up from seemingly nowhere. Tracing the steps backward to their cause, if possible, may help but only afford a partial understanding. Rushing to understand may lead to a logical but erroneous conclusion. The fragments may be all that can be grabbed during the split second lag time between our body receiving stimuli from the field and it being diverted either to consciousness or unconsciousness. Most stimuli never reaches consciousness says science journalist Tor Norretranders. "Each second, our consciousness reveals to us a tiny fraction of the 11 million bits of information our senses pass on to our brains. Most of the information from our senses goes to our unconscious. Trust your hunches and intuitions—they are closer to reality than your perceived reality, as they are based on far more information."[11]

Trust is important but not as a blind leap of faith. Trust is best when grounded in the energy of the body. In this way it is easier to stay connected to what matters, to feel our rhythmic flows, to discern if the hunch, intuition, and sudden imaginal appearance is the body speaking to us with our best interests in mind.

A few questions to consider:

- Can we enter the shadow region with integrity without rushing to conclusions?
- Can we connect in a genuine and humble way to the core and balance of being?
- Can we uncover a path of creative expression, healing, and interconnection?
- How does our perception tie into a habit, pattern, or a breakthrough?

The unconscious exerts influence without our awareness like a software program operating in the background. It's the shadow that traces our steps. It's the backseat driver whose steering wheel periodically renders ours ineffective. The unconscious influences thought and action, word and movement often without our welcome. But actively engaging the imagination while rooted in the body, we learn to grow toward heightened wakefulness, the eye seeing what the hand cannot feel, the hand touching the unseen, senses in sublime and extraordinary collaboration. *(Exercise 5:7 Shadow Moves)*

Getting Under the Skin

We may want to choose our thoughts and craft expression with care. Thoughts influence our well-being, including the health of our cells, a reason Bruce Lipton suggests that we watch what we think. It is inadvisable as well as impossible to make conscious our 11 million bits of information, the overload overwhelming our senses and impeding our functioning. We can be selective however, which is why active imagining is important. With our best interests in mind, active imagining puts the steering wheel in our control, a veering around the detour sign rather than turning back, the light of our somatic investigations and awareness minimizing shadows. Rather than passive recipients of experience, we are creators. We exercise choice. We determine direction and content. We decide when to exert effort and when to ride the waves. We welcome doing and being, constantly adjusting for balance, clarity, curiosity, and growth. Testing the limits of comfort, ease, and risk, we explore what is possible when we show up with wonder to a line of writing or sequence of motion. We find ways to delight our cells, each breath, sensation, and thought harmonizing with the nervous system.

The activity of deliberate imagining, similar to play, provides a rich opportunity to test boundaries and try new behaviors. As a laboratory for pursuing inquiries, it supports engaging with the mysteries and complexities of life. In active imagining, we apply a structure to see what shows up. We set parameters and guidelines. We may hold to a time frame and include props. We select a narrow or broad focus. The container of our inquiry should support feeling free to challenge notions or explore the edges of consciousness, to jump or make a fist, to dabble with and pursue an inclination, to write with a wriggling hand about the heart tremors that rattle our chest ever since falling off a friend's horse or to stomp the floor. We practice full body listening. We invite and investigate unfamiliarity alongside the familiar. We pursue a physical inquiry to probe images and sensation. We focus on the resonance of a gesture, a word or phrase. We center ourselves in the moment and loosen expectation and the usual controls. We practice wonderment and whim, forwarding momentum with laxity. We improvise. We follow a body rhythm. We let it carry us to rocky and wooded terrain, to cells and cellulose,

5. The Imagining Body

creation in its moment of unfolding, our life pulse on the front line in play. This breath, then another. This movement and moment unfolding, then another. This word, then the next. *(Exercise 5:8 Touching the Cells)*

Engaging the imagination intentionally, like writing from the body and being somatically aware, ushers in a heightened way of being with greater access to ourselves. We need not operate by familiar guidelines—although we may—but can extemporize. We can probe if what is possible can become probable. Human development author Joseph Chilton Pearce writes: "Physiologically superior to ordinary 'eye-seeing,' imagination comes in from higher up the 'evolutionary stream' of vision, and even employs a higher, purer form of light.... Rather than the senses impacting the mind with imagery, as in ordinary seeing, through imagination the mind impacts the senses with imagery."[12]

We imagine by engaging the body in motion and word. We imagine the life pulse informing our flesh. We imagine ourselves in balance with our mind and body. We imagine reclaiming our body for its highest purpose. We imagine for the sake of the emergence of new life.

Not in certainty but despite certainty, we befriend the unknown. We invite presence in emptiness. We establish balance and when it's lost, stimuli crowding our attention, we establish it again, resting our head on the pillow of equilibrium. We repeatedly turn to feeling the body which is always rooted in the present moment. We look at motion. We look at emotion. We look at them shaping our body and influencing perceptions and decisions. We feel into our matter.

What is now? What arises into awareness?

Here dwells an edge. Here in this moment life unfolds, the unknown pressing against the known, discomfort and disorientation mixing with excitement and curiosity, the past chafing against the present and leaning into the future. What takes place in the clashing of forces may appear unfamiliar or confusing. Or full of clarity. Whichever way, ride it out. Abstain from judgement. Proceed with an open bodymind. Be curious and alert. Squirm if needed. Write drivel. Put pride on pause. This is your personal time, a sacred time, where putting on airs is unnecessary. Instead, honor the life pulse. Follow breath. Tune into sensation, to the movie of the mind and the unwitting moves of the body. Feel. Let go of expectation. Witness what arises. Be your own best audience and confidant. Be yourself in flow.

If grace takes place, great! If awkwardness take place, that's great, too, and may indicate avoidance and resistance, material to play with further. Contact improvisation cofounder Nancy Stark Smith calls the moment of awkwardness the gap, a space often accompanied by discomfort. Sticking with the awkwardness, not denying it, allows it to undergo its natural growth process that supports learning and embodiment.

Carry on. Let go the need to be right and in the know and welcome the yet-to-be named or identified. This is a liminal space, a threshold between here and there, the known and the unknown. Here is creativity birthing form, a butterfly pushing against its cocoon, not yet aware it no longer crawls nor is about to flutter. Here form and awareness merge, life doing what life does, writhing, expanding, recanting, sputtering, and stepping out. The body reveals its wondrous generative process, the matter of our flesh and knowing repatterning and building upon the core design of our life.

The Synergy of Moving and Writing

The type of imagination and embodied knowing born from combining writing with moving has a rare potency. Each practice alone stirs the imagination, but their combination creates a synergy, the blend larger than either part alone. One furthers the articulation and awareness of the other. Their synergy carries us past the edge of knowing into new feeling and insight. Its expression is not solely cognitive, but a deeper felt experience which creates a somatic opening. We are stirred to notice the inexplicable. We are stirred to opening.

Creative energy comes in waves, bursts, and nudges. It broadens the horizon and brings the previously missed into focus. It may appear for no obvious reason. We may feel compelled to move a certain way, to pursue an image or phrase, to tie expression to our breath or experiment with resistance.

We don't know what we know until the waves and particles are translated into a familiar language, until it reveals itself as image, word, sensation, or emotion, and we investigate it through writing, and moving with awareness. The process furthers the event, prolongs our engagement with the material, and gets us perceiving and feeling anew.

The combination offers an investigative path, a somatic journey for entering the body that take us where we might not have access otherwise. We go because engaging the life pulse reconnects us to the vitalizing creative current. We go because connecting to the core of our being is empowering and liberating. We go because any refusal blocks the life pulse and diminishes well-being. We assume active and passive roles, welcome blur and focus, an inhale and exhale, all in intimate engagement with creative energy and our life pulse.

We follow a word lain path. Phrase after phrase ushers in the present in revolt against pretense and an embrace of the now. We follow the momentum of word after word in an uncensored stream. We stand in the light of thought, no expression reproachable but as feast-worthy as any banquet of possibility. We allow. We seek. We pilot and drift with the dream of our imagination. We let it take us on a journey. We welcome the motion of our arms and the press of our fingers as they alter the space within and around us. Our body moves. We sit taller. Vertebrae elongate. We feel beat, vibration, saliva and sweat. We calm down. We see firsthand how every action and thought has consequences and rise to the occasion of putting forth authentic expression toward our ever evolving self. We follow turns of thought and motion to see where they lead. We follow ourselves. We lose ourselves in words and the body, one phrase slipping into another, one gesture replacing the next, each one yearning for the light of day, not immediate understanding, but an unmediated, direct sense of embodiment.

The parade of words and movement alters us. We notice their shapes and shifts, how each moment in the intimacy of its infancy, in its tries of balancing then with soon. We are a parade of words. We are language incarnated.

We let our movements demonstrate on page and space what becomes us. Flesh and breath, ink and page. Words arise. Movements arise. Being takes center stage. Usual controls relax. Connections emerge where before there were fragments. Fragments emerge where before there were untenable connections.

We are finding out, fleshing out. We are the matter of what matters, learning to what degree we have choice.

Exercises

Exercise 5:1 Invitation to Imagination

- Come up with and write a definition for imagination. How often do welcome it into your day? Why or why not? Imagine how it might better nourish your life.
- Underline a phrase or image from your writing that sticks out or appeals to your for whatever reason.
- Assign it a location in your body. Root the image there.
- Imagine its changes. Move with those changes. Feel or watch those shifts.

Exercise 5:2 Healing with Imagination

- Choose a physical or emotional part of you that needs healing. If it's the latter, assign it a location in the body.
- Describe the ailment. Listen deeply to that part of your body. Ask your body why it has manifested this ailment. For what purpose?
- Give it an image or motion that could be useful in shifting it toward healing. Either let it arise on its own or deliberately come up with one.
- Notice any judgements around this imagining. Notice any fear.
- Write freely about what comes up.

Exercise 5:3 Cellular Breathing

- Lie on a flat surface. Let the weight of your body give into gravity and relax.
- Take several full inhalations and exhalations.
- Begin to listen for a hum or feel a subtle vibration.
- Let your arm or leg or torso spill into a new position and relax with several cycles of breath. Listen for a hum or subtle vibration.
- Spill into another position and deeply listen and relax.
- What do you notice? If you are having difficulty sensing the cells breathing, use your imagination.

Exercise 5:4 Words and Motion Arising

- Sit quietly and allow your body to be still. Begin to do a Body Scan (see Exercise 3:3 for a reminder of how to do this.)
- Look for the presence of a word in your body. It may hover in the muscles of your neck or the bone at your elbow.
- Once you've located your word, notice the area of the body in which it was found. How would you describe the area around it?
- Write down the word and the description of that area.
- Do a 10 minute Free Write using that word and the descriptors.
- Underline a phrase from the writing that holds appeal to you for whatever reason.
- Find ways to translate the phrase into movement. Use a part or the entirety of your body to do so. Use the phrase as a movement prompt. Let it carry you to consequent moves. Let it carry you away, periodically returning to the original phrase.
- Write about your movement experience or continue the movement experience verbally.

5. The Imagining Body

Exercise 5:5 Manifesting with Embodied Symbol

- Choose something in your life that you want to manifest, for instance, a new job or improved health.
- Come up with a symbol for it.
- Come up with a movement that corresponds with the symbol.
- Embody the movement and symbol. Feel the image in your limbs and torso and see it with your inner vision. Repeat, then vary the movement. Let motion evolve on its own. Follow the story and dream of your body.
- Notice your breath.
- Write about what took place.
- *Variation*: Write the story of your manifestation. Notice what images appear in the writing. Use those images to move.

Exercise 5:6 Transformative Image

- Write about what it means to transform. What image do you use to enable growth? What is a North Star that guides you?
- Choose an area of your life that you want growth. Come up with and a symbol that can shift your awareness and take you to the next place. Write about it.
- Come up with a movement that represents that symbol. Explore the symbol through movement. Use your entire body or a part. Use active imagination.
- Write about what took place.

Exercise 5:7 Shadow Moves

- Choose a habit of yours that you don't know why you do it. For instance, it could be biting your nails or feeling tired when you perform a chore.
- Embody that habit. Move it. Let it take over. Exaggerate the motion. Make it smaller and larger. Relocate it to another place of your body.
- Come up with an attitude to accompany the movement, for instance, annoyed or sad. Come up with another attitude. Continue with an attitude that feels compelling.
- Let the movement and attitude lead. Experiment, improvise, and play.
- Write about what you noticed while moving.

Exercise 5:8 Touching the Cells

- Make a list of negative beliefs you hold about yourself. Make a second list of positive beliefs you hold about yourself.

- Choose one of the negative beliefs and lie on the floor. Where does that belief reside? Move that part of the body.
- Choose one of the positive beliefs and lie on the floor. Where does that belief reside? Move that part of the body.
- What difference in sensation and feelings do you notice in doing both?
- Rephrase the negative belief into a positive. Locate it in your body and play with the motion that arises.
- Upon completion, rest in stillness on the floor.
- Consider rephrasing all of your negative beliefs into a positive.

6

The Evolutionary Body

In the late '90s, I taught in Malaysia for a program that enabled Malaysians to earn an American degree. Students attended all classes on their home turf until the final class in which they traveled to Ottawa University in Kansas. Volunteers who lived alone and had an available room generously offered housing to students. Without meeting the students beforehand, these volunteers generously welcomed strangers into their home and provided meals and a bedroom. These gestures were well-intended, however, they didn't receive the appreciation expected. What they did was expose a cultural blind spot.

Though recognizing their host as kind, many students talked about how lonely and sad they felt. They couldn't understand why their host would choose to live alone and felt particularly distressed by being given an unshared bedroom. By contrast, they were familiar with living with parents and siblings, perhaps an aunt and uncle, extended family dwelling next door or a few houses away. Meals, too, were a shared affair. Family regularly spilled into available spaces at any hour. A student may study on a couch in the living room beside a parent drinking tea beside a sibling watching television. The more family in your space, the merrier. This was the Malaysian way of sharing. For them, the collective body matters.

Americans, on the other hand, prize individuality in all its forms. The preference is to have one's own bedroom, to live alone, and own a car, all considered status signs. We prefer to come and go as we want and not have to compromise our desires. We prefer to get into our car that is not shared and rest in the privacy of our home that is not shared. Although sole car and home ownership as status signs have shifted in recent years, particularly among the Millennial Generation, we still relish signs of individualism. The more we can distinguish ourselves and set ourselves apart from family and community, the better.

Somatic awareness fits into this individualist belief system. In getting to know ourselves and unearthing subjective experiences for their gems, we strengthen our individuality. We learn what distinguishes us from others. We learn how to transform a weakness into a strength, how to heal wounds, and how to feel into our depths and celebrate the wonders of our body. We learn how to use them to our benefit. We find out to what degree we're unique, idiosyncratic, and similar. Great, I say. Celebrate those distinctions and idiosyncrasies and similarities. Accept each and every one. Learn from all of them. They are indeed the route to embodied empowerment and growth. But if we believe somatic awareness solidifies separation and individuality, then we have yet to ask essential questions concerning our physical inquiry and mistakenly believe our somatic exploration complete.

There's more. Much more. As much as we distinguish ourselves, we are never fully apart. The collective body is with us at all times, influencing us at the same time we influence it, an unstoppable relationship of interdependence, a We. We are droplets in the same ocean of humanity. We are one inhabitant among innumerable inhabitants of Earth. We are in a constant sustenance dance with the ground and water and air, all of which is essential for survival. For this reason, it's not only important that we take care of our body, but that we similarly attend to the environment. Not only are we nourished by the ground and water and air, we are the ground and water and air. Says ecofeminist Susan Griffin, "We know this earth is made from our bodies. For we see ourselves. And we are nature. We are nature seeing nature."[1] The air we inhale becomes us. The water we drink becomes us. The earth that

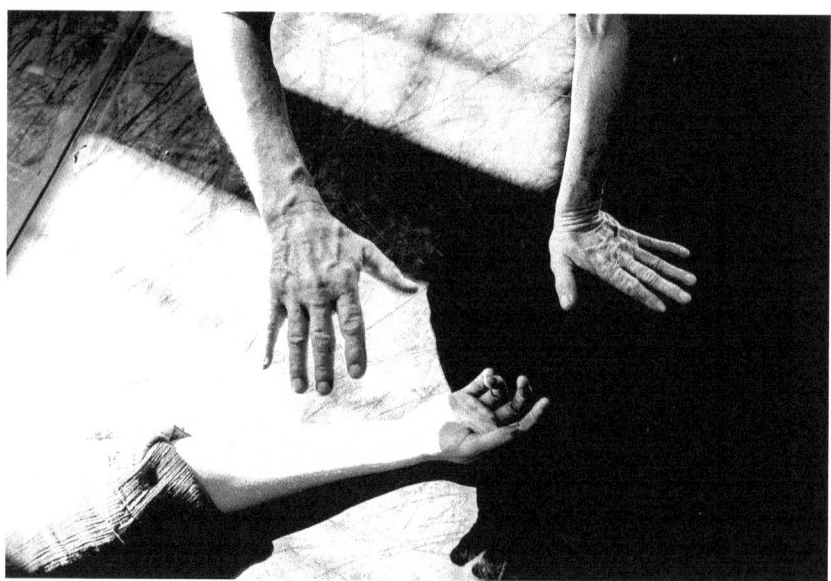

Somatic, relational connecting

grows the food that we eat becomes us. Conversely, the hair loosed from our head becomes the nest for a sparrow. The carbon dioxide we exhale is converted into oxygen by trees. Upon death, our dust is food for earthworms and other critters.

Such ideas are central to deep ecologists who refute the commonly held western idea of exploiting the earth for human consumption, a hierarchical relationship that places humans above all else. Instead of being anthropocentric, deep ecologists are holistic. They recognize that all forms of life are to be honored, that the health of the Earth is inextricable from the health and well-being of bodies, rocks, rivers, bees and bears. Astrophysicist Carl Sagan takes the idea a step further to include all matter and space. He says, "The cosmos is within us. We are made of star-stuff. We are a way for the universe to know itself."[2] *(Exercise 6:1 The Directions)*

We are interconnected. My motion effects how you move. How you move affects how I feel. How I feel influences how you feel or move or think. Together we create a lively field of influence. Among the biological events taking place are the firing of mirror neurons. Authors of a study on the physiological and cognitive influence of dance on an audience report that a "dynamic inter-subjective activity such as dance" activates mirror neurons in the motor cortex. "The confluence of bodily movements, gestural expressions, and rhythm—whether observed by an audience or performed by dancers—is able to imbue the participants with feelings and emotions that compose the aesthetic experience of dance."[3] Similarly, energy practitioners recognize the mutual influence of the biofield. They work with both the visible body and the energy body that extends beyond the skin to strengthen and heal a client. This mutual confluence is perceivable once we turn attention toward it, once we still ourselves long enough to notice the activity in the margins of our awareness. *(Exercise 6:2 Give and Take)*

Total separation is impossible.

The impossibility of absolute separation

We are not as isolated as we think we are, the wall of our thoughts and skin highly permeable. To believe in impenetrable boundaries is to exile a substantive perception concerning our vitality and prosperity into a personal shadow. Many westerners who have subscribed to the notion of individualism ignore the evidence of our collective interaction. They position individualism as a pinnacle of achievement and dismiss the reality and benefit of the collective. Denying the latter fills the collective cultural shadow with ideas essential to our survival and minimizes our collective potential.

The collective shadow can be as or more problematic as the individual shadow, the havoc of one multiplied by the many, a near total eclipse. An idea repeated often enough inches its way into believability. A crowd of naysayers are capable of trampling upon the ideas and experiences of a few.

But not always. Fortunately, a more complete somatic investigation recognizes the inquiry of one as interdependent with the many. It is a dynamic balancing act of voice and vision and matter in all its forms. It is a recognition of the mutual influencing that takes place beyond our skin.

Social Somatics

We all do our best at life management. Some of us are caught in survival mode. Political, social, or personal circumstances delivered a fate of hardship. The day is weighed down by finding and affording food and a safe environment and quelling the anxiety, pain, and insecurity that comes with hunger, the absence of a stable home, and uncertainty about the future. The more fortunate among us are graced with going to work and receiving a paycheck, sharing a meal with family or friends, engaging in a movement practice, journaling, and falling into bed for a restful night of dreams.

Social somaticists Martha Eddy and Carol Swann recognize that somatic practice is never a solo practice and encourage actions that intentionally support the collective and social body. Social somatics "uses awareness of cultural complexity and contexts of privilege and oppression to engage in creative and embodied action … to bridge disconnections and transform cycles of injustice into new paradigms of mutual respect for all."[4] Social somaticists may get involved in building an alliance of migrants and domestic workers to inform them and increase their rights. Social somaticists may get involved in a community getting access to healthy food which minimizes the illnesses associated with the substandard food, sometimes the only food available to those living in areas considered food deserts. They recognize that the well-being of an individual body can be determined by the actions of a group.

Historically, somatic practices were frequently group practices. Court dances, for instances, reminded participants about their social role and accepted behavior within the culture. Among indigenous populations, group ritual for important events such as a hunt, harvesting, and marriage frequently included dance, music, and storytelling and reinforced community ties and ecological communion, honoring nature and each other as central to any ceremony.

Collateral damage from conveniences brought about through industrialization and modernization is isolation and disembodiment. We've moved away from an agrarian sensibility and connection to the land into factories and business parks with cubicles. The lights from stars and moon are obstructed by the fluorescence of a city which impacts circadian rhythms and release of melatonin. Looking up, if we even remember to do so, stops at the urban ceiling. We are controlled by the workaday 9-to-5 schedule, not our own personal, bodily timing. We are dissuaded from visiting our neighbor a cubicle away and forging collaborative ties. A restorative nap or stroll outside can be misconstrued as insubordination and useless idling and cause for employment termination. We abide by hierarchies that position one or a select few at the top who issue rules that everyone else is expected to follow. We are a cog in a corporate machine, a worker on an assembly line of capitalism expected to follow the rules of the game. For most of us, neglecting our needs day after day takes its toll on our health. When a culture doesn't promote genuine self-care, many of us end up disembodied, sleep deprived, stressed, anxious, unhappy, and lashing out at each other. We are not encouraged to explore our potential but pressed to fulfill an expectation based on external factors.

Social somaticists promote a holistic perspective. They engage in actions that value deep democracy, an idea originating with Arnold Mindell. The principle of deep democracy values all voices, the majority not privileged above the marginalized. Deep democracy recognizes that for businesses, government, and social groups to perform at their highest potential, they must honor the truths of all. This perspective poses a challenge when another's truths runs counter to our own. Too readily, we fall into dualistic thinking, an either/or stance that refuses to see any value in an opposing view.

Social somaticists recognize that every part plays a significant role in the smooth running of the whole, that it is in everyone's interest to establish alliances and cohorts. They recognize that activity upstream always flows downstream. What affects the personal affects the interpersonal. What impacts others impacts us. The health and well-being of a society depends upon the health and well-being of all its citizens. To listen and attend to the voices of another is to listen and attend to oneself.

A natural offshoot of this principle is empathy, an element of emotional intelligence. Empathy allows us to see with the eyes of another, to feel with the heart of another, to understand the perspective of another. Empathy reinforces collaboration. A leader who takes in the needs of others inspires them to perform well. Social somaticists believe that by bringing up those in struggle, you bring up all, each member in a group a valuable player. Their performing well raises the bottom line.

We may prefer an exclusionary hold onto the notion of self-reliance and individualism, believing that for there to be a winner, there must also be a loser or that self-reliance and individualism cannot coexist with interdependence. These limited ideas reveal a myopic understanding that inadvertently feeds the cultural shadow. Just because we can't see the persons downstream, in the next room, or on the other side of the ocean doesn't mean they don't exist and can't feel our influence. This idea is not meant to encourage subscribing to a new belief system without examining it first. An untested replacement of one idea for another is problematic and reinforces disembodiment. Knowing comes through embodied first-hand experience. Research an idea while also trying it on. Feel how it scratches personal biases. Reflect on the materials that may contribute to discomfort. Be reminded that the ego typically prefers to be right, even when it may be wrong, and is susceptible to overlooking key information that yields a more complete picture.

Like it or not, we are all interdependent. The smoke of your cigarette wafts through the vents of my apartment building to where I stand at the stove steaming vegetables grown forty miles up the road at an organic farm that receives water from the river downstream of a manufacturer of stainless steel pots like the one I'm using and claims their water discharge is clear of toxins.

Or another example: From dancing, writing, and meditating with somatic awareness for decades, I have established a degree of ease.

A simple gesture impacts others

That ease shows up in my walk, speech, and presence which clients and students frequently comment on, readily detected when we're in the same room. "As soon as I walk into your space," says my client Amy, "my stress starts dissipating. Is there some way to pack you up and take you home?" My ease lowers their anxiety which allows them to handle work and family challenges better and access the vitalizing energy critical to their interests and needs.

Watch any group of people long enough and witness the coordinating of body rhythms and movements, or entrainment. Influence and interdependency work in both directions. One person crosses her legs which prompts another to do the same which prompts another across the room to rest his head in his hand and so on, an impromptu series of unconsciously executed choreography. This is only what's visible. Under the cover of skin, a similar dance is taking place physiologically as brain waves, pulse, and a host of chemical reactions respond in a corporeal give and take. Interestingly, if a group intentionally coordinates their movements and surrenders oppositional energy, they achieve neurosynchrony, brain wave harmonization. The coordination is neither mechanistic nor forced but embraces the breath and breadth of those involved. They typically experience an uplifting and unifying feeling, a sense of belonging and mutual support, the mind of a group of people united in purpose. Similarly, research psychologist Orme Johnson and others report that when a large group of people meditate, the coherence of their brain waves is said to positively influence those who live nearby, a phenomenon referred to as the Maharishi Effect.[5] *(Exercise 6.3: Synergetic Waves)*

Thriving in Radiant Aliveness

We are all doing our best. To navigate life challenges with work, family, and health, we survive as best we can. My interest is in moving past a winner-loser, predator-prey, me versus you paradigm. Keep an eye on the sympathetic nervous system that cues us to danger and the route to safety, food, and shelter but also engage the systems responsible for higher mental functions. Support biological and social systems that make us all winners. Support systems that are mutually beneficial and sustainable. Support systems that allow us to thrive.

Thriving includes heightened awareness, creative expression, embodied presence, and a balance of conscious drives with unconscious impulses. Thriving recognizes that the home of our flesh matters greatly for all of us. Thriving acknowledges through personal experience that awareness extends beyond the border of our skin and identifies self as interconnected not only with fellow people in the same room but people throughout the building and across the globe. We are individuals as well as members of a family, community, tribe, congregation, race, and species interconnecting with countless humans and nonhumans. Thriving includes health, well-being, sustainable actions, and long-term vision for all living beings residing on this earth that provides us with food, water, air, and home.

Thriving, at its best, leads to radiant aliveness. Radiant aliveness is the embodiment of the liberating energy that underlies our psychological and cultural biology. It is us in harmony with the splendor and misery of every circumstance, each greeted as an opportunity for being and growth. It is us in harmony with whatever arises in this moment. Radiant aliveness arises most frequently while I am dancing, writing, meditating, or any combination thereof, my body tingling and glowing. It begins with a focused concentration on myself engaged in the activity and shifts to me radiating outwards. Like the concentric circles made by a stone skipping the surface of water, the self I identify as me spreads toward an unseen shore. Awareness of interconnections follows, me a continuation of all else, me in mutual support of all that is, a oneness that is euphoric. Writing about it in prose falls short in capturing the experience because radiant aliveness doesn't coincide with the logic of common grammar and syntax, a reason for expressing it in poetry and dance. Radiant aliveness relishes contradictions and anomalies, each phrase in movement or dance unfolding subsequent revelations.

Radiant aliveness simmers and transcends separation. It is marked by a free flow of me with you with other with knowing and feeling and relaxing and standing against or in favor of wind and words and the heat of an idea meeting matter. This moment, then the next. This feeling, thought, movement, then the next. This moment with us present and awake.

The bodymind is continuously betwixt and between. Think polysemously. Feel synaesthetically. Stand with an awareness that gravity holds us in place, but our place is in constant motion, orbiting the sun along with 7.5 billion fellow humans and an infinite number of atoms and cells upon a planet suspended in an unfathomable universe. At the moment, I can't picture the immensity of it all. My head strains with my paltry glimpse of such an insurmountable task. I would rather watch the cardinal that just flew across the back yard, uncross my legs, and take a deep breath. I would rather type this sentence.

This, however, is its starting point: awareness, followed by a sense of spaciousness.

Radiant aliveness is an abiding both with and beyond subjective/object, me/you, inside/outside dichotomies. The personal perspective is perceivable by a choice of attention, but so too is the domain of We, an intersubjective space, an interconnected field that contains subtle energies, visible and invisible forces in play, a group or culture's ideals, the resonance of personal and collective knowing and joy, and the resonance, too, of personal and collective discomforts and denials. The intersubjective space is the meeting ground where subjective influences collide and mingle, where relatedness and relationships form, where life sourced within finds another personal perspective, another body, another subjective system.

The intersubjective space is a We-space resulting from two people, a group, or an entire population, depending on where the boundary and the limits of perception is placed. Our predilection for individualism and belief we end at our skin means overlooking and taking the wilderness of the intersubjective space for granted. We don't know what lives in the field between people nor do we know its benefits. We are too often cornered by own beliefs and fears to look any further.

Despite its close proximity to our physical body, this We-space often remains remote, undeveloped, and unintegrated. The pervasiveness of chronic loneliness with its ties to widespread depression suggests that many of us have yet to tap into this region, that we have let ourselves be ruled by fear. We have yet to reach out across the divide. How to connect to another in a meaningful, satisfying and transformative way leaves us baffled. Given how many of us are disembodied, unable to connect within, it comes as no surprise that we fail at co-embodiment. We have yet to validate the existence of this shared field, this shared energy, let alone explore it. We have yet to look over our shoulder and across the room for a supportive community. We have yet to discover the creative forms of collaboration which may provide necessary solutions to the many urgent social, political and environmental problems we currently face. We have yet to employ deep listening collectively. *(Exercise 6:4 Intersubjective Presencing)*

I would call not for an ideal-

Sharing the field of the intersubjective space

ized vision of this shared field, however well embellished, but welcome a creative, emergent and expansive expression of presence that is inclusive, integrated, and radiant. This field of presence relies on the synergetic possibilities arising from deep respect, honesty, and genuine collaboration. It relies on grounded knowing and contains a degree of risk. We allow ourselves discomfort and vulnerability and the fullness of our breath. We welcome shadow, dark matter, and also light. We open. We allow. We connect beyond the usual channels of perceptions. We rely on sensory information and take ourselves to the next level. We not only survive, we thrive.

When we engage in radiant aliveness which includes acknowledging the intersubjective region, our nervous system hums along with digestion and other systems, hormones, breath, and cells emanating in a vibrancy of efficiency. We are not beholden to static patterns, energy blocks, and anxiety which contribute to disease and breakdowns in social systems, but adapt to the moment's ebb and flow. We embody waves of being, a cellular vibratory massage, the very motion that births neuroplasticity. According to neurologist Rebecca Gladding, when we refocus, break habits, and heighten awareness, achievable through somatic practices, the brain rewires. Weak circuits are replaced by healthy ones. Perspectives shifts, not as a replacement or negation of the former, but as a progression of awareness and values. Radiant aliveness practices balance on all fronts, personal, physiological, social, and political. We evolve. In accordance with an intimacy with our being, we do so naturally, a neurogenesis bloom. The inner world is experienced as an extension of the outerworld or, conversely, the outerworld is experienced as an extension of the innerworld.

Radiant aliveness emanates a vibrant life supporting field. Its embodied presence promotes balance with all life. Its concern is to continually engage with sun and cells, atoms and air, unearthing and composting every hue of light and shadow. It celebrates the body as process for increased consciousness, embodiment, and life at its optimal expression. It represents the incarnation of the life force constantly adjusting for balance and dynamic homeostasis. It is the in breath and the out breath that relies on the lungs of the universe. It is the embodied presence of one magnified by the presence of many. It is the life impulse expressing itself and taking an evolutionary step. *(Exercise 6:5 Emanating Radiance)*

Evolving and Emergent Potential

Thriving welcomes creativity and innovation as a necessary reflection and adaptation to changing circumstances, indicators of psychological, emotional, physical, and economic health in continual adjustment to the needs of people. A wide range of intelligences are utilized as fits the circumstances. Expression and utility are welcomed, not at the expense of a particular demographic, but in support of the whole. Thriving recognizes that a healthy personal life pulse is reliant upon a healthy collective pulse and a healthy earth pulse, a complex vital partnership that honors biological, seasonal, ecological, and planetary cycles. Thriving recognizes subtle changes as ongoing, unstoppable, and synonymous with growth.

We move in concert with continual change. Every moment, uncountable cells die and are replaced, one thought drifts into another, and the Earth continues its orbit around the sun, affecting temperature, climate, and moods. Slowly we evolve. It's not a complete departure of one perspective for another but an emerging developmental shift in touch with the vital web of life. Grounded in our embodied self while simultaneously holding multiple perspectives is a sign of health and strength just as diversity in plants and animals indicates a healthy ecosystem, each player interacting with fellow biotic and abiotic players, the living and nonliving, all performing essential roles.

Too much stasis and homogeneity impedes well-being and is a denial of natural life cycles. All elements, not only a few, keep a body or a system operational. Remove one and watch the system weaken, erode, and possibly collapse altogether. Researchers exploring connections between intestinal bacteria and ailments such as anxiety, depression, obsessive-compulsive disorder, ADD, autism, and Alzheimer's disease suspect that diverse gut bacteria, our microbiome, is essential to the breakdown of different types of food.[6] Our gut is a microcosm of our participation in larger systems. In solving a life challenge, a multiplicity of perspectives helps root out oversights and weakness to make our best step forward. Diversity is an indicator of strength as is complexity.

Evolving includes complexity. Evolving is a developmental term that comes from the Latin "evolvere," which means to unroll, roll out, roll forth, and unfold and was used originally in reference to books and later adopted the additional meaning of developing by natural processes to a higher state. The term "evolution" came to be aligned with biology at a time of adhering to notions of dualism, mind versus spirit and science versus religion. A somatic perspective moves past dualism and points out that evolution is much more than our biology. It entails our psychological, cultural and spiritual development, the entirety of our bodymind. That development is not passive, but one we cultivate actively and consciously.

Evolution is an inclusive developmental growing. No step negates the previous step. Rather, one precedes and is reliant upon the other. We cannot get there, wherever there is, without first being here, wherever here is.

To evolve, we aim to see as much of the picture as possible, both our personal perspective and multiple angles of truth, perspectives considered welcome as well as those deemed unacceptable. Somatic explorations which rely heavily upon subjective experience are a reminder that truths are many and diverse. Our perspective is a single point in a complex, multi-layered pattern, a colorful mandala of desires and disappointments, experiences and ideas, systems humming and stalled, lives perched at the precipice of birth and death.

Embodied presence is a radical act of awareness and growth. Embodied presence leads to the discovery of options resulting from knowing who we are and acting from that awareness. Embodied presence comes from contemplating our conditions, accepting what needs acceptance, and taking steps.

Embodied presence opens us to elasticized time. The common clock-centric time of chronos expands into kairos, time sensed as an endless now. With kairos, we enter a liminal space that relaxes usual perceptions of time and space. Habitual behaviors are paused and dropped as if a faraway summoning captures our attention and we stop current activity to investigate. Less compulsive and obedient to the demands of chronos, we position ourselves at a threshold between here and there, this and that. Distinctions that previously cornered us conceptually loosen. If writing, the words carry us line after line, the world dimensionally revealing itself. If moving, the subtle shifts of motion delve deeper into nuances of stretches and contractions, each position and breath leading to new awareness. Previous conclusions peel away layers of truths and untruths for the birth of something yet unknown in the process of its becoming. We are positioned at the precipice of flow and pulse, particles throbbing in quantum universal play.

At the precipice we discover choice. We discover that the sensations, emotions, impressions, and memories that shape who we are, that we have identified thus far as us, are not fully what they seem. Depending on how they're measured, we are more or less than their amalgamation. In this deep embodied listening, we see we've absorbed, imitated, and reacted to many conditions of our lives and realize that none of them need define who we are. Our body is more malleable and fluid than any one definition, an awareness that once embodied provokes growth. Here is the breath of change. Here is us riding an evolutionary wave. There is no going back. There is only forward, that is, if we embrace the life impulse and align ourselves with the natural cycles of health and living.

Higher States of Consciousness

Engaging in embodied presence, we integrate shadow material into consciousness and celebrate embodied radiant aliveness as an evolutionary act that is pivotal to our well-being, and by extension, the perpetuation of our species, and the vitality of Earth. Anything less is devolving. Anything less hastens our demise. We may prefer to hear what we want to hear, what coddles reason and alleviates fears, but it may be neither what saves nor exalts us at the end of the day.

To increase consciousness and evolve, to develop and embrace the emergence of our potential, Integral philosopher Ken Wilber, who developed a comprehensive map of consciousness after studying dozens of models from around the world, suggests we plunge "into authentic higher states of consciousness—such as meditative states—then the faster you will grow and develop through any of the stages of consciousness. It is as if higher-states training acts as a lubricant on the spiral of development."[7] Developing and experiencing higher states of consciousness are worthy goals, but they must be inclusive and holistic, mind and body equally honored. A meditative higher state of consciousness needs, in particular, to take matters of the flesh into account. An expanded consciousness based solely on thought, as occurs with spiritual bypassing, is vacuous, a hollow vessel devoid of the animating force of the life pulse, the body missing in action, the flesh immaterial, an oxymoron with detrimental repercussions. The shadow, not our developing, grows. To avoid spiritual bypassing, it helps to connect somatically with motion, stillness, and embodied language. A creative practice positions us on the front line of existence with all of its awe inspiring mysteries. A creative practice tied to a somatic practice roots us in our body and beyond our body. We arrive at embodied knowing, embodied feeling, and embodied presence, an arrival that is ongoing and infinite. (Exercise 6:6 *Core Evolving*)

Flesh matters. Life happens. Focus comes and goes. Awareness flickers off and on. Consciousness embraces unconsciousness, giving both a stage, alerting us to pain, joy, pleasure, and choice, pointing the way to expression, knowing, well-being, truth, and beauty. We open to the depth and expansiveness of being present. We resonate with What Is.

None of this is easy. Nor should it be. Suspect what's easy. Suspect, too, what is difficult. Challenge assumptions. Challenge the beliefs held close to the chest and the ones pushed to the far corner of the room. Challenge how meaning is reached. Challenge any predisposed interpretations of experience. Explore what your body is saying and what shies away from being said. Understand how your somatic practice heightens awareness of words and concepts and motion as they arise from your flesh and how they enter your body from pages, mouths, and bodies afar. Let life move you. Recognize biases. Step into another's orbit. Rotate in place and time. Be still amid motion. Be who you are and welcome your becoming. Feel the breadth of your being.

Those who are intimate with the body sense the inner world colliding with the outer world. We find the words and movement that fit us. We let them point to us and carry us outside. We let them disorient and clarify us. Says dance therapist Mary Starks Whitehouse, "Movement to be experienced, has to be found in the body, not put on like a dress or coat. There is that in us which has moved from the very beginning; it is that which can liberate us."[8]

Words and concepts, too, must be found in the body. Says Helene Cixous about writing,

> As soon as you let yourself be led by codes, your body filled with fear and with joy, the words diverge, you are no longer enclosed in the maps of social constructions, you no longer walk between walls, meanings flow, the world of railroads explodes, the air circulates, desire shatters images, passions are no longer chained to genealogies, life is no longer nailed down to generational time ... you are returned to your innocences, your possibilities, the abundance of your intensities. Now, listen to what you body hadn't dared let surface.[9]

Determining fit or flaw, authentic or forged, makes the difference between affirming or denying our very becoming. We get to inhabit ourselves in ways that are ordinary and extraordinary, that connect us deeply to ourselves and to the larger world. We see the role we play in our own as well as the larger narrative, our skin encapsulating us and touching what resides beyond immediate reach.

In honoring the creative force of the life pulse, present in all living things, we practice a deep listening to self and other. Philosopher Jean Houston refers to this force which wants nothing more than to be itself, to be seen and heard, and to realize the fullness of its existence as entelechy. Says Houston, we need

> to tap into a symbolic or archetypal expression of the entelechy principle operating in our lives. Entelechy is all about the possibilities encoded in each of us. For example it is the entelechy of an acorn to be an oak tree, of a baby to be a grown-up, of a popcorn kernel to be a fully popped entity, and of you and me to be God only knows what.... We feel its presence as the inspiration or motivation that helps us get life moving again after times of stress or stagnation.[10]

The objective of the entelechial force is to fulfill purpose, to embody being and our highest expression of existence. Consider it an invitation to thrive.

An inhabited body puts us in intimate contact with purpose tied to environment. Done with expanded consciousness, we are situated in the ground of being and becoming, the forces of the universe at our finger tips. The world moves through us. The world speaks to us. We are moved and speak up, in awe of happenings all around, coursing up our spine, sparking ideas, motivating action, or generating a stillness as steady as a mountain.

Creative energies are coursing through us at all times. Actively engaging such energies and tying them to heightened states furthers those states since the rules of creativity abide by blending an uneasy alliance of chaos with order. Creative expression is the manifestation of the life pulse, the awe of creation coexistent with destruction, opposing forcing living side by side, overlapping, entwining, pushing, relaxing, and pivoting. Creative expression is the unfolding of awareness, of breath taking form, of a body in languorous recline on a chair rising into grace, a flock of words lifting the bodymind to its next horizon.

The Spirit Body

Thus far, I have omitted any discussion about religion and spirituality. Understandings and the practices of them both are so broad, varied in meaning, and divisive, they mislead and harm sometimes more than they help and uplift. Religion typically involves an alignment to hundreds or thousands of years of dogma. Spirituality is frequently understood as avoiding the hallowed halls of religious institutions and emphasizes a more personal relationship with a chosen god, or gods or goddesses. Too readily we argue over which group has access to the truth—typically mine, not yours—and we rush to conclusions—again, mine, not yours. What many of us overlook is acknowledging how the particulars of our spiritual intelligence influences our beliefs and experiences. We may be blind to our degree of spiritual literacy and see it as fixed rather than developing. Ken Wilber sees us readily interpreting our spiritual state of consciousness, such as having a peak or religious experience, according to our stage of consciousness and using the same words for wholly (pun intended) different experiences.[11] What results is confusion and stepping on each other's spiritual toes.

My intent is not to critique specific religions. I do want to bring attention to what many hold in common, their view of the body as inferior. The body is often construed as the site of all things vile and sinful, to be denigrated, controlled, and transcended for a heavenly bodiless realm. Transcendence involves the divine existing outside us and suggests that until we detach from the body through subjugation, disparagement, or death, we cannot move on to a higher, better place. Separation from and contempt toward the body, which leads to disembodiment, is welcome and considered a lofty, perhaps the loftiest of all divine aspirations.

To transcend, however, a body is a necessity. It is the very vehicle of practice. Without the body there can be no existence whatsoever. To deny the body is a type of delusion, a dissociation, akin to defining the ocean without mentioning fish, coral reefs, and tides. One needs the other. One is a continuation of the other.

Many of the dominant religions are patriarchal and dualistic, men wielding power over women who, in some instances, have little say. Amanda Williamson and others, editors of *Dance, Somatics, and Spiritualities*, recognize how problematic it is to discuss religion and spirituality whose language is steeped in "male-centered, heterosexist, and imperialist religion ... lodged in conceptions of socio-cultural repression and ideological dissociations of body, mind and spirit [that] denigrate the body, flesh, nature, women and immanence."[12] These editors call for an expanded understanding of spirituality and the pivotal role of the body.

Unsurprisingly many somatic practitioners provide a view of divinity which includes the body, all bodies, gender deemed as unimportant. Body-Mind Centering therapist Linda Hartley recognizes that her practice wasn't developed for spirituality, yet she has used it for this purpose. She says it has been "a door opening into the deeper levels of ourselves and others and the universe in which we live, helping us to place our individual lives within a greater context of spiritual life."[13] Somatic practitioners such as Hartley believe that divine states are achievable through a deep and balanced rooting in the flesh, in a grounded body that welcomes creative expression, and allows hidden and dormant energies to be revealed. Yet patriarchal attitudes aim to control the Earth, the body, and women whose close alliance with nature is visible in biological cyclical processes such as menstruation. Until we slid down the birth canal or were removed via C-section, our very existence depended on our mother's health. All of us without exception were once part of a woman's body.

Despite this momentous relationship, sexist attitudes often discount embodied ways of knowing and experience, often sidelined, debased, and omitted because they are associated as feminine. Full embodied knowing does not discriminate based on gender. Full embodiment is an awareness of all that is, our body alone and in relationship, our body influenced by upbringing, geography, economics, political climate, and much more. A somatic perspective recognizes divine awareness arising from a deep listening to the entire body of flesh—any body, your body, or mine. Embodiment is crucial not only to the development of our spiritual intelligence but also to

6. The Evolutionary Body

evolution. This process, this rooting within, grounding, centering, allowing, and creating, promotes a rising up, an inspired upwelling, a divine immanence.

Immanence suggests the divine is already within and awaits our discovery. It resides in the heart, gut, and mind, in our thoughts and in our motion. Rather than refer to body or bodymind, a more apt term may be bodymindspirit. From a somatic perspective, the within extends also to an exterior, given that borders are porous. The divine, therefore, also exists in the air, ground, and water, further extending the definition of body. Cosmologist Brian Swimme goes yet another step and refers to the cosmos as having consciousness, everything inextricably connected, a cosmic spirituality. Consciousness is a fundamental building block of the universe. He says,

> [E]ach being in the universe is an origin of the universe. "The center of the cosmos" refers to that place where the great birth of the universe happened at the beginning of time, but it also refers to the upwelling of the universe as river, as star, as raven, as you, the universe surging into existence anew. The consciousness that learns it is at the origin point of the universe is itself an origin of the universe. The awareness that bubbles up each moment that we identify as ourselves is rooted in the originating activity of the universe. We are all of us arising together at the center of the cosmos.[14]

Access to immanence occurs with a point outside us, within, or in the shared unitive intersubjective field. Our body is the most direct and only path to the divine. Through awareness of our body, we awaken to what is already present.

What is present is a weave, an overlap, the pulse of breath and blood, the pause between thoughts and memory, the spine aligned, the body leaning against a tree whose roots spread to a neighbor's yard adjacent to a field that juts up against the sea whose waves splash skyward. What is present is what exists between us, trees, atoms, heat, rivers, and stars, the very same matter that comprises us. What is present is effortless perfection, the body in repose or in fear, prose that dances limb by limb, heart by health, cells by sun, the earth seeing sky, the story of you touching the story that is me.

Just connect.

This connection is kosmocentric. "Kosmos," from Greek, recognizes the universe to include matter, body, mind, and spirit. Connect with breath, word, motion, memory, body, earth, and sky. Kosmocentrism is linked to panpsychism, a word originally used by philosopher Francesco Patrizi in the sixteenth century. Panpsychism is the belief that all matter has consciousness, a radical and far-reaching idea that is being explored by neuroscientists such as Christof Koch and physicists such as Roger Penrose. Philosopher David Chalmers considers the idea that "[E]very system is conscious, not just humans, dogs, mice, flies, but even ... microbes, elementary particles. Even a photon has some degree of consciousness ... some element of raw, subjective feeling, some primitive precursor to consciousness."[15]

Pansychism raises numerous provocative questions: How do we define consciousness? How do we define mind and matter. How do we define body? Attempts to answer these questions typically mire us in dualism. Discussion inevitably turns to differentiating matter from spirit or energy, religion versus science, and mind versus body. Defining and understanding by their very nature tends to separate one experience from another. A somatic approach, on the other hand, reaches toward understandings that are syncretic and holistic, an embrace of, for lack of a better word, the bodymindspiritenergy. We are an indivisible cocktail whose ingredients and amounts continually change. We are a confluence of fields. We are subject merging with object. We are emergence and awareness.

Just connect. Entering at any one point provides access to the entirety. Start with deeply listening to your body.

In writing with the sensed body, moving with embodiment and with body soaked words, being still and being in motion, we come to knowing, to feeling, to animating, and to integrating anew. We engage in a somatic practice to right a wrong, to find out, to shift into a new position, to heal, resolve, create or because to do anything else but this pleases us to no end. We delight in the light, in presence, in radiance.

Moving and listening close to the bone and breath and linking words to somatic journeying uncovers What Is and what wants to be, experiences inside and outside, sides numbering more than two. We inquire and feel into what is, imagine yesterday and today, step forward and land in our evolution. Truth motivates us. Ease motivates us. Pain motivates us. Creativity motivates us. Beauty motivates us.

Words and motion reach into the silence of our body. Silence and stillness reach into the recesses of our flesh. What exists in the interstices of known and unknown, the body still and the body in motion, influenced and influencing, is a moment ripe with potential.

We have no time. We are time.

In flow, in the unitive, borderless field, we are capable of integrating the many forces always at play. In pause in breath in body, we are capable of integrating the many forces always at play. Repeat yourself. Don't. Revel in your being. Move, write, do, be.

Listen closely. Listen deeply within. Listen to what calls your name and calls you by another name. Follow the wave of a hand and motion so subtle you might shrug it off. Go there. Go where your body moves you.

Exercises

Exercise 6:1 The Directions

This exercise can be performed with any number of people.

- Staying within your continent, stand facing North. Welcome memories of people, places, and activities that took place in the North. Notice any sensations in your body as you stand in this direction.
- Turn to face East. Welcome memories of people, places, and activities that took place in the East. Notice any sensations in your body as you stand in this direction.
- Turn to face West. Welcome memories of people, places, and activities that took place in the West. Notice any sensations in your body as you stand in this direction. Notice how they differ from those of the East. Notice if you stand differently, hold more or less tension in your face, or anywhere else in your body.
- Turn to face South. Welcome memories of people, places, and activities that took place in the South. Notice any sensations in your body as you stand in this direction. Notice what memories and sensations are unique to this direction.
- Repeat the directions, however this time, each person taking a turn to briefly mention one of these memories. Notice what memories and sensations are unique to this direction.
- Repeat the directions, however this time, leave your continent and reflect on any events that may be taking place there.
- Stand in the direction of your birth place. Then look up beyond the ceiling, into the sky, then into the stars.
- Write: Carry out the exercise above standing in all directions. Write about a pivotal person, place, or activity associated with that direction. As you write, be aware of how you body experiences the direction.
- Write about what you heard someone share about a given direction, its impact on you, and how it compares to an experience of yours with that direction.

Exercise 6:2 Give and Take

This exercise is to be done in pairs.

- With elbows bent, raise your hands palms out facing your partner. Notice the sensation from the muscles required to keep your arms in position. Notice any other sensations and thoughts arising.

- Without touching, slowly move your hands closer to each other. Look for heat, tingles, or any energy coming from their hands and yours.
- After a few minutes, move your hands to meet those of your partners. Find a palm to palm position that allows each of you to remain grounded and centered in your own body. Shift your body as needed to avoid strain.
- Notice sensations entering your hands and traveling throughout your body. Notice how those sensations effect balance and comfort. Notice what thoughts and emotions arise.
- Take turns initiating small movement without verbally informing the other about your movement. As the leader of movement, be spontaneous. As follower, do your best to follow the cues and direction of the leader. Both of you remain grounded and centered.
- Stop initiating and let movement arise on its own. Neither of you lead. This may take some time. Be patient. Let the life pulse assert itself. Follow where it takes you.

Exercise 6:3 Synergetic Waves

This exercise is best done by a group of 3 to 6 people.

- Stand in a circle with several inches of space between you and your neighbor. Ground your energy.
- As you continue standing, notice the unintentional movements you do to maintain your position. Notice the same in others. Notice facial expressions, twitches, angles of neck and pelvis, shifts from one leg to the other, and any other movements.
- Mirror some of the movements and repeat them a few times. Eventually it will be unclear with whom the motion started.
- Allow stillness to occur if that takes place.
- Allow movements to enlarge and be exaggerated.
- Watch for the emergence of group motion synergy. Let it emerge on its own.
- What does it feel like when all or most are doing the same motion? When all are doing their own movement?

Exercise 6:4 Intersubjective Presencing

This exercise is to be done in pairs.

- Sit across from a partner.
- Set a timer for 10 minutes and one of you report on what you sense arising within you. Observe what is taking place through each of your senses. Observe, too, emotions and thoughts. With each observation, say, "I am sens-

ing...." Refrain from telling a story or explaining your observations. Meanwhile your partner listens impartially.
- Switch roles.
- Allow for quiet before resuming.
- Set a timer for 10 minutes and one of you report on what you observe in the space between you. Allow a free flow of observations of activity arising in the intersubjective field. No need to be concerned if you're doing it right or wrong. It's okay to speculate and imagine, for instance, especially if you've never done anything like this before.
- Switch roles.
- *Variation*: Respond via movement. Transfer each observation into an immediate movement.
- Write about what took place. Reflect on the activity. *Variation*: You may also want to continue presencing via writing.
- Discuss your experience with your partner.

Exercise 6:5 Emanating Radiance

- Sit, lie, or stand in a comfortable position.
- Imagine an orb, star, or another symbol that represents radiance. Imagine it at the center of your brow emanating outward. Connect with your breath. Each round of breath grows the orb.
- Imagine another at the center of your heart emanating outward. Grow the orb with your breath.
- Imagine another at the center of your lower belly emanating outward. Grow the orb with your breath.
- Let each center join to create a larger one. Grow the joined orb with your breath.
- What do you see, hear, feel? Notice what you notice.
- Let each emanation gently work its way to the outermost part of your body.
- Let the emanation fill the room. Let any thought and judgement dissolve.
- Gently let the emanation go beyond the room to the entire building, outside the building and beyond.

Exercise 6:6 Core Evolving

- Write answers to the following: What does it mean for you to evolve? What is your definition? Where is your core, a central area of energy that contains the potential for an evolutionary shift? Place your hand intuitively on that spot now. Why there?

- Complete the following sentences: What is core to my personal well-being is _____. What is core to collective and intersubjective well-being is _____.
- Write your intention for this exercise to include a benefit for yourself and for more than yourself.
- Come up with a movement and a written phrase that represents your core.
- Freely explore them in writing and in movement. Allow flow.
- Write about the findings of your exploration.
- Using elements of this exploration, create a structure with 5 steps that includes your initial movement and written phrase and furthers the journey of your evolution.
- Carry out your structure. Be open to what shows up.
- Write about what took place and/or write from a specific part of your body.
- *Variation*: With a small group, once everyone has completed their individual explorations, the group together comes up with a structure to further a collective journey that includes parts of everyone's individual exploration. Discuss after the structure is carried out.

7

The Practicing Body

This section offers a variety of exercises for delving further into your somatic body and increasing your ability to listen deeply, to move, write, and foster awareness. I titled this chapter with the word practice. Practice emphasizes ongoing activity, that to do an exercise once is insufficient. Learning and growing takes place from repeating an activity, noticing what changes and what remains the same. A practice provides a frame or structure for perceiving. Any one of the exercises in this chapter and throughout the book may become a regular part of your practice.

The aim of the exercises, like the others throughout the book, is to provide structures and guidelines to enter your body for accessing your expression and wisdom. Some exercises include explicit step-by-step instruction while others are more vague and open. There are multiple ways to do any of them correctly, however, the approach of greatest significance is your own personally meaningful investigation. Find your way. Move and write through hunches and doubts, through pauses and flow. Accept when output trickles and when it surges.

If you've gotten this far in the book, my suggestions are familiar. Follow energy and attention. Go with more or less carefulness than is your habit. Go slower or faster than you might otherwise. Welcome the familiar and the odd, targets reached and missed. Notice what is obvious and what hides off to the side. Notice what makes you flinch and what ignites ease. Notice your rhythms, how you balance and center, and when you are knocked off. Proceed with compassion and curiosity.

Veer off course if you feel compelled to do so. Your energy has a wisdom that awaits your learning. You best uncover the wisdom and insights of your somatic body. Let it take you on a journey.

At the start of each exercise, clarify your intention. (See *Exercise 1:6 Intention* for details). Recall that intentions are the north star, there to guide you through an experience that may be disorienting. A well thought out and concisely written intention helps to set hoped for actions and results into motion. There is no guarantee of a particular outcome however. An expectation may be more hindrance than help. Intentions clarify thinking and launches energy necessary for manifesting. At the completion of the exercise, revisit your stated intention and compare it to what took place.

7:1 Body Telling Patterns

- Come up with categories for the body based on objective or subjective. They may be anatomically or psychologically based. Below are several possibilities:
    - Systems: skeletal, muscular, nervous, endocrine, cardiovascular, immune, respiratory, digestive, urinary, reproductive
    - Digestion: mouth, tongue, esophagus, stomach, small intestine, large intestine, anus, pancreas, live, gallbladder
    - Endocrine Glands: adrenal, hypothalamus, pineal, pituitary, thyroid, thymus, pancreas, testes/ovaries
    - Regions of Pride or Shame: hair, eyes, muscles, knees, nails, heart
    - Regions of Weakness: knees, upper right arm, digestive system, lungs
    - Injuries and Surgeries: knees, lungs, ankles

Grounded and aiming skyward: Amy Impellizzeri

- Choose a category for exploration. Familiarize yourself with the location and function of the body parts in that category.
- Place your hand on that region. Rest it there for several breaths. What sensations and feelings do you notice?
    - What memories are connected to that region? What images appear?
- Do simple movements with attention focused on that region. Consider shifting weight, making small waves, contractions, and stretches. What do you notice? What sensations, feelings, images and memories surface?

7. The Practicing Body

- Tell a story by writing *about* or *from* that region as it relates to the category. You may want to consult Exercises 4:5 and 4:6 to recall differences in the narrative styles. What patterns do you see? How do those patterns help or hinder you.

7:2 Opening the Body

- Make a list of ways to categorize levels the body. Below are possibilities. Add to the list ones that resonate with you.

Physical Body	Energetic Body
Spiritual Body	Movement Body
Physiological Body	Emotional Body
Intuitive Body	Shadow Body
Creative Body	Mythic Body
Storied Body	Flow Body
Cosmic Body	Evolutionary Body

- Choose a body you'd like to access.
- Write freely about your definition, understanding and experience with this body.
- Underline 3 phrases from this writing. Use them to prompt a movement exploration.
- Write about what took place. What images, sensations, feelings, movements, and memories were elicited?

7:3 Activating Energy Centers

Various schools of belief place centers of integrative power in various regions of the body. These centers, sometimes referred to as chakras, are typically accompanied by a cross section of nerves associated with a particular gland. Experience activating a center yourself. Notice which ones shift your consciousness and engage your strength and which feel neutral. Imagine the centers as a sun, star, or wheel that radiates energy.

7:3:1 Activating Breath

- Locate a center where you feel breath. Stay with it to note the time needed to complete an inhale. Note the inward pull and how its influences nearby areas. On the out breath, notice the same. What areas of the body move as breath is released?
- Send the breath to a place where you believe breath doesn't reach anatomically. Imagine breath, for instance, arriving at your toes. Wiggle each

slightly to receive breath. Map a route from the bottom of your body upward, stopping in at least 5 areas.

- Feel breath circulate across your back, each shoulder blade spreading on inhalations. Imagine yourself a falcon or another admired bird opening its wings. Feel the energy stirred. Note what sensations and images arise.
- Breathe several rounds, each time deepening the inhalation and fully emptying yourself on the exhalation. Stop if you get dizzy.
- Write about what you noticed. While writing, maintain a focus on breath. Or write from breath, each phrase deepening and easing breath.

7:3:2 Activating Heart

- Put your focus on your heart. Feel the space that occupies the central upper area of your chest.
- Inhale and welcome expansion. Leave your attention there for a few minutes noticing what you notice. Imagine your heart engaging breath and an energy exchange. Invite it to expand and contract. Invite light and color.
- Slowly raise your arms. At shoulder height, extend arms outward. Then slowly bring your arms in. Repeat the motion outward and inward several times.
- What images arise? Invite light and color.
- Lay on your back on the floor and extend your limbs including your head. Use the image of a star fish. Take turns reaching with each limb. Lie on your side and do the same. Contract your belly muscle for strength.
- Write about what you noticed. As you write, maintain a focus on heart region. Or write from the heart, each phrase furthering the heart's opening.

7:3:3 Activating Solar Plexus

- Put your focus on your solar plexus located at the base of your ribs.
- Extend your arms while aware of strength emanating from this region. Invite light and color.
- Lay on your side on the floor and extend a leg and make scissor movements while aware of strength emanating from this region.
- Write about what you noticed. As you write, maintain a focus on the solar plexus region. Or write from the solar plexus, each phrase furthering its opening and strengthening. Or write from solar plexus.

7:3:4 Activating the Sacral Plexus

- Put your focus on your sacral plexus located a few inches below your naval.

- Stand with your legs a few inches apart, knees slightly bent. Slowly rotate your hips as if hoola hooping or making the figures 8.
- Rock your pelvis forward and backward.
- Write about what you noticed. As you write, maintain a focus on the solar plexus region. Or write from the solar plexus, each phrase furthering its opening and strengthening.

7:3:5 Synchronizing Energy Centers

- Place your focus on the crown of your head. Imagine a flower bud opening. Take in several easy breaths.
- Place your focus on your brow. Imagine a flower bud opening. Take in several easy breaths.
- Place your focus on your throat. Imagine a flower bud opening. Take in several easy breaths.
- Place your focus on your heart. Imagine a flower bud opening. Take in several easy breaths.
- Place your focus on your solar plexus. Imagine a flower bud opening. Take in several easy breaths.
- Place your focus on your sacral plexus. Imagine a flower bud opening. Take in several easy breaths.
- Place your focus on your perineum. Imagine a flower bud opening. Take in several easy breaths.
- Variation: Once placing your focus on each area, invite a word or phrase to arise and write it down. What is a common theme of the writing? In what ways do they relate to each other? What is the narrative thread or story?

7:4 Words Prompting Movement

Below is a mix and match list for prompting a movement exploration. The list is not intended as complete. Feel free to add your own.

Movement

wiggle	undulate	stretch	straighten	bend
unfold	contract	expand	jump	fall
rise	squirm	crawl	gallop	fly
strut	wince	run	shake	gyrate

Ways to Move

softly	cleanly	strongly	sensually	vulnerably
unpredictably	hypnotically	awkwardly	flamboyantly	gently
heavily	directly	fluidly	nervously	meditatively
courageously	spastically	smoothly	fast	slow

- Choose a word from Movement and one from Ways to Move. Improvise and explore the combination. Choose a few others including ones you may have come up with.
- Write about your experience.
- Variation: Write using any of these combinations.

7:5 Varying Breaths

- Ground your energy.
- Focus on your natural rhythm of breath.
- After several rounds on natural breathing, slowly take in a longer, deeper breath. Fill your entire torso with breath before slowly exhaling, taking longer than usual. Repeat several times.
- Return to your natural rhythm for several rounds of breath.
- Decrease the time for each inhale and exhale. Pull breath it and push it out. Repeat several times. Return to your natural rhythm if you get dizzy.
- Assume an easy rhythm.
- Do simple movement in accordance with your breaths. Exhale with expansive motion, inhale with contractions. Do slow movements with slow breaths, fast motion with fast breaths.
- What do you notice?
- Variation: Do the same while writing.
- Variation: Write about your experience.
- End by grounding your energy.

7:6 Journeying

A journey is much more than getting from one place to another. A journey recognizes the importance of experiences and perceptions along the way. A somatic journey invites you to listen deeply and to unravel a habit or block in favor of opening to new energy.

7:6:1 Door Walk

- Go for a 10 minute walk in an urban environment.
- Each time you encounter a door, pause at the door. As you stand, notice any somatic responses and write the first thoughts that comes to mind. You may choose to write about the shape and color of the door, how you imagine the door used, who last walked through, or any other objective feature or subjective reflection.
- As you resume your walk, notice your posture, sensation, and memories.

Which sense is dominating? What happens when you switch to a less dominant sense or underdeveloped intelligence?
- Upon completion, compose writing using all of your writing.
- Variation: Respond in movement. Each time you encounter a door, pause at the door and notice any somatic responses. Move with the prompt of those somatic responses. Later compose an entire dance based on your movements.
- Variation: If you live in a rural area, instead of doors, come up with another cue such as sycamore trees or hooting owls.

7:6:2 Insighting

- Come up with a question in search of an answer or insight. For instance, you seek to better understand your choice of a romantic partner, you falling short of a career goal, or want to determine a path toward health.
- Come up with 2 gestures and a symbol that represents your quest.
- Choose 5 locations. They could be outdoors, indoors, or a combination.
- Visit each location. Perform the gestures and the symbol. Linger at the location. What do you notice? What sights, sounds, images, sensations, emotions and memories capture your attention?
- Continue movement and engaging with what you notice.
- Upon completion, write about what you noticed. What happened that was expected or unexpected? In what ways did the gestures and symbol evolve?

7:6:3 Brushing Away Stress

- Stand or sit and ground your energy.
- Come up with a word or an image that represents what is stressing you.
- Make brushing movements. Brush with your hands against your body and in the field around you to remove the stresses.
- Come up with another word or image that represents what is stressing you.
- Do a few rounds of breath. Invite breath into your torso and along the spine.
- From the center of your body, slowly extend awareness outward. See and feel a porous sheath that protects you and maintains your ease.
- Notice any stimulation coming in through your eyes, ears, nose, and skin.
- Variation: Instead of doing the brushing movements, write in a brushing off way.

7:7 Sounding into Writing

- Find a space where noises from outside will not interfere and you feel free to make your own noise. You may do this exercises sitting or lying down.
- Make sound by focusing on vowels. Let them ride your breath. Repeat the sound. Vary your volume. Watch how they vibrate your mouth, esophagus, head and other regions. Notice any effects of those vibrations.
- Make sound by focusing on consonants. Notice the parts of your mouth needed in their pronunciation, for instance, how the lips purse or the tongue presses against the teeth. Repeat the sounds while noticing how they vibrate your head, throat, chest and other regions. Vary your volume.
- Make other sounds with your mouth, expressive exclamations as well as phonemes from other languages.
- Play and experiment with sounds with childlike curiosity.
- Let go of restraint. Follow your body's impulses toward sounding. What emotions are stirred? What images arise?
- Let the sounds tumble into a word. For instance, f-f-f-f may become fundamental. As you pronounce the word, emphasize each phoneme. It may come out as FUN-da-da-da-men-tal-l-l-l.
- After several minutes, resume silence. What sensations do you notice?
- Write for several minutes. Silently begin with sounds until a word emerges. Once a word emerges, let it tumble into an entire sentence. Let the sentence tumble into another sentence. Do not think. If you find yourself thinking, return to making phonemic sounds until a new word, then sentence tumbles out.
- Read over your writing without making any corrections. What odd phrases and words did you generate? What emerged in the process? What is newly revealed?

7:8 Furthering Writing

Writing can get us caught in intellectualizing and distancing us from voice, character, action, and flow. Embodying and feeling the resonance of words is essential to cultivating inspiration and imagination and creating compelling work.

I distinguish between writing meant for craft and writing meant for truth. Either can be compelling. Craft involves studying, reading, and abiding by and furthering or breaking with established writing forms and norms. It aims for a sense of beauty, a loaded word I am purposefully leaving undefined in favor of your definition. Truth is unconcerned with craft. It aims to transfer experience of the present into an honest expression with little concern for beauty. Its strength comes from the power of its emotive resonance.

A third option is combining both approaches and finding a satisfying balance. Determining how much of each is an art, another loaded word I am leaving undefined in favor of you being an authority with your own values and guidelines.

7:8:1 Flowing through Writer's Block

Recall the power of your thoughts, a reason to reframe a block as a pause or any other word of your choosing. The blocked material needs to dip into the pool of the fermenting unconscious before coming up for air. Sometimes after a few days, the block dissolves on its own. Other times, the process takes too much time and we can't afford to wait. With this in mind, consider the following:

- Define your block. What is its color? Dark red or dystopia pink? What is its texture and shape. Hard as block of granite? Does it have opossum sharp nails? Write as many details as possible.
- Come up with an action that can transform it.. For instance, the dark red may need a spill of white. The hard granite may need shattering. The opossum may need food. What seems appropriate given what you've written? There is no wrong answer. Your reply is an entry.
- Now do a body scan (see Exercise 3:3) to assign the block a location in your body. If it's location it not readily apparent, assign it a location.
- What other features do you notice about the block in that location? Send breath to that location. Move from or with that location in a way that feels natural and represents the block in some way. For instance, red may suggest quick movements. Granite may suggest contracting your entire body, tucking your arms and legs into a ball. Note your responses to the movements.
- Now do the transforming action. Take your time. Go as slowly or quickly as is needed. Notice your breath and any sensation or images that appear. Explore through movement. Use active imagination.
- Write about what took place.
- Variation: Continue the quality or character of your movement in writing.
- Variation: Your entire being is the block. Come up with a shape and motion that characterizes it. Hold the position as if you are a painter's model in stillness. Get to know the block through deep listening, your inner and outer eyes.
- Move as needed. Surrender to the block's impulses.

7:8:2 Writing Truth

- Ground your energy. Seated, place your feet firmly on the floor, hands on the desk, spine elongated. Take several easy breaths.
- Write only that which you can write. Write with ruthless honesty. If the only word that comes forth is "crap," write it over and over and over again, repeating until exhaustion.
- Make sense or make no sense. Write close to the bone and the cells. Write from the biofield.
- As you write, notice repercussions of the writing on your body. Periodically pause to follow the resonance of your words.
- Write about what you notice.

7:8:3 Developing Character

- Write as much as little or as much as you know about the character you're developing. What would this person wear, eat, drink? What position does this person use to sleep? How does this person sit and walk across the room? What are some of their mannerisms, for instance rubbing eyes or sitting cross-legged.
- Embody this character. Imagine yourself as this person. Imagine yourself wearing their clothes. Assume this character's way of sitting and walking across the room as they might. What does this person do? How do they breathe or stand? Is their body stiff or pliant? What do they notice in the environment and within their body?
- What information about this character is useful?

7:8:3 Developing Voice

- Breathe into the gut. Feel that area. Write from a voice of the gut.
- Breathe into and feel the heart. Write from a voice of the heart.
- What other region of your body could you voice? Write from that region.
- Write with all of these voices. Welcome them all into the room. Let me them have a conversation.

7:8:4 Developing Rhythm

- Come up with a movement pattern. Repeat it over and over. Get comfortable with it. Embody it from feet on up.
- Continue the rhythm in words.
- Come up with another movement pattern. Repeat it over and over. Get comfortable with it. Embody it from feet on up.
- Continue the rhythm in words.

- Come up with a more complex pattern. Mix it up. Keep it going for several minutes.
- Continue doing the same in words.

7:9 Cultivating Peace

What follows are a series of contemplative practices for instilling calm and centeredness. They combine motion and image with a focus on deep listening. Find a way to move with and feel what subtle energy they impart. There is no wrong way to do them. Find your way. Adjust the movements as needed. Explore what provides energizing calm. They may done alone or in a group. Upon completion, write about your experience or write from the state each stanza provokes.

Move like a wind gust.
Step like raindrops.
Celebrate the glee of parched earth drinking.
Ground in Being.

* * *

Lift arms to heart opening heaven.
Rotate pelvis in orbit of calm.
Ignite a small fire along the spine.

* * *

Toss pebbles of doubt and self-denigration.
Inhale the air of nurture, sun, and bloom.
Whirl in delight.
Root in stillness.

* * *

Clasp your head in embrace of unity.
Open your heart in embrace of love.
Blanket your belly in embrace of vitality.
Steady both hips to stand in a brilliant beam of renewal.

* * *

Breathe like a child.
Breathe as your favorite color.
Breathe as winter, spring, summer, fall.
Breathe in the presence of a beloved.
Breathe through the landscape of your skin
into the quiet hollow of every cell.
Breathe with the universe's radiant glow.

* * *

Glossary

action—a consciously constructed activity intended to create a structure for exploration
active imagination—a technique developed by Carl Jung that transforms contents of the unconscious into images, narratives, and other perceivable phenomenon.
awareness channels—a perceptual path
biofield—the electromagnetic patterns of energy that permeate our physical body and commingle with similar fields outside us
bodymind—the inextricable tie between the body and mind, one entwined with the other
body scan—an viewing and inventorying of the internal body to increase awareness
deep democracy—an attitude that focuses on the awareness and equal importance of voices that are both central and marginal.
deep listening—sensing that involves eyes, ears, heart, and mind, providing information about the somatic body
embodiment—a state of being that includes an interplay between body, spirit, and world
inner sense—sensing that goes beyond the usual sense organs and includes intuition.
intelligences—abilities and knowledge divided into specific modalities or skills
intersubjective space, or **intersubjectivity**—an interconnected field that contains subtle energies, a group or culture's ideals, the resonance of personal and collective knowing and joy, and the resonance of personal and collective discomforts and denials
kinesthesia—awareness of the visible motion of the body.
life force—vital current of subtle energy coursing through us and throughout the universe. Different cultures referred to it as qi, chi, and prana
physical inquiry—an intentional somatic exploration or investigation
proprioception—the ability to sense the interior environment of the body, specifically its motion and location, in relation to the external environment.
radiant aliveness—the embodiment of the liberating energy that underlies our

psychological and cultural biology and emanates a vibrant life supporting field.

resonant writing—an approach to writing that acknowledges and makes use of the reverberating influence of language upon the body

sensory awareness—focus based on any of the senses

social somatics—the study and active experiences generated that take into account context and culture for holistic models centered on physical experience

somatic attuning—an ongoing practice of checking in with our body and performing a felt sensory inventory and bringing the internal world in sync with the external world

somatic literacy—detecting and understanding the body's signals

somatic opening—a disruption in bodily functioning and awareness that leads to new understanding

somatics—the field of study dealing with subjective bodily phenomena

subtle energy—the life force, sometimes referred to a chi or prana, that courses through our body and the environment

we-space—a type of collective awareness, the subtle energy shared between people

Chapter Notes

Introduction

1. S. Brown and L. Parsons, "Learning, Arts, and the Brain," *Neuroeducation*, https://www.giarts.org/sites/default/files/Neuroeducation_Learning-Arts-and-the-Brain.pdf, 2008, accessed April 27, 2016.

Chapter 1

1. Thomas Hanna, "What Is Somatics?" *Bone, Breath, & Gesture*, edited by Don Hanlon Johnson (Berkeley, CA: North Atlantic, 1995), 341.
2. Hanna, 342.
3. Octavio Paz, *Convergences: Essays on Art and Literature* (San Diego: Harcourt Brace Jovanovich, 1987), 66.
4. Hanna, 348.
5. James Joyce, "A Painful Case," *Dubliners* (London: Penguin Classics, 1983), 85.
6. My somatic opening led to my involvement with dance and an ongoing involvement with contact improvisation that resulted in my book *Contact Improvisation: An Introduction to a Vitalizing Dance Form* (Jefferson, NC McFarland, 2006).
7. Martha Graham, *Blood Memory: An Autobiography* (New York: Doubleday, 1991), 4.

Chapter 2

1. Scott Edwards, "Dancing and the Brain," *On the Brain*, http://neuro.hms.harvard.edu/harvard-mahoney-neuroscience-institute/brain-newsletter/and-brain-series/dancing-and-brain, accessed January 28, 2017.
2. Joe Martino, "A Neuroscientist Explains What Happens to Your Brain When You Meditate," *Collective Evolution*, June 15, 2014, http://www.collective-evolution.com/2014/06/15/a-neuroscientist-explains-what-happens-to-your-brain-when-you-meditate, accessed April 25, 2017.
3. Brigid Schulte, "Harvard Neuroscientist: Meditation Not Only Reduces Stress, Here's How It Changes Your Brain," May 26, 2015, https://www.washingtonpost.com/news/inspired-life/wp/2015/05/26/harvard-neuroscientist-meditation-not-only-reduces-stress-it-literally-changes-your-brain/?utm_term=.8d1d61335540, accessed December 3, 2016.
4. See his *Frames of Mind* (New York: Basic, 2011) for a complete explanation of his ideas.
5. Danah Zohar and Ian Marshall, *SQ: Connecting With Our Spiritual Intelligence* (New York: Bloomsbury, 2001), 7.
6. Consider *Working on Yourself Alone: Inner Dreambody* as well as *The Leader as Martial Artist*.
7. Deane Juhan, *Job's Body: A Handbook for Bodywork* (New York: Station Hill, 2003), 43.
8. James Oschman, *Energy Medicine in Therapeutics and Human Performance* (Boston: Butterworth Heinemann, 2003), 61.
9. Daniel Goleman, *Primal Leadership: Unleashing the Power of Emotional Intelligence* (Cambridge, MA: Harvard Business Review, 2013), 275.
10. Don Childre and Howard Martin, *The HeartMath Solution: The Institute of HeartMath's Revolutionary Program for Engaging the Power of the Heart's Intelligence* (New York: HarperCollins, 1999), 100.
11. Michael Gershon, *The Second Brain: A Groundbreaking New Understanding of Nervous Disorders of the Stomach and Intestine* (New York: Harper Perennial, 1999), 8.
12. Haruki Murakami, *IQ84* (New York: Vintage International, 2013), 36.
13. William Blake, *The Marriage of Heaven and Hell* (CreateSpace, 2014), 17.
14. Moshe Feldenkrais, *Movement for Actors* (New York: Skyhorse, 2002), 5.

Chapter 3

1. Deborah Hay, *My Body, My Buddhist* (New Hanover, NH: Wesleyan University Press, 2000), 2.
2. Graham, *Blood Memory,* 16.
3. Rumi, *The Essential Rumi* (New York: Harper, 1995), 175.
4. Jack Kornfield, *No Time Like the Present: Finding Freedom, Love, and Joy Right Where You Are* (New York: Atria, 2017), 13.
5. Bruce Lipton, *The Biology of Belief* (London: Hay House, 2008), xv.
6. Daniel Siegel, *Mind: A Journey to the Heart of Being Human* (New York: Norton, 2017), 313.

Chapter 4

1. Pico Ayer, "Writing Undoes Me," *Lion's Roar,* November 1, 2005, www.lionsroar.com/writing-undoes-me, accessed April 7, 2017.
2. Celeste Snowber, *Embodied Inquiry: Writing, Living and Being through the Body* (Rotterdam: Sense, 2016), 9–10.
3. Graham, *Blood Memory,* 4.
4. Audre Lourde, *Sister Outsider: Essays and Speeches* (Berkeley: Crossing, 1985), 36.
5. Clarice Lispector, *Agua Viva* (New York: New Directions, 2012), 17.
6. Rosanna Greenstreet, "Q&A: Margaret Atwood" in *Guardian,* October 28 2011, https://www.theguardian.com/lifeandstyle/2011/oct/28/margaret-atwood-q-a, accessed March 19, 2017.
7. Paul Auster, "Jonathan Lethem Talks with Paul Auster," *Believer* www.believermag.com/issues/200502/?read=interview_auster, accessed December 15, 2016.
8. Catherine Pearson, "The Benefits of Writing with Good Old Fashioned Pen and Paper," *Huffington Post,* September 12, 2014, accessed April 13, 2017.
9. James Pennebaker, *Writing to Heal: A Guided Journal for Recovering from Trauma and Emotional Upheaval* (Oakland, CA: New Harbinger, 2004), 18–26.
10. Mihaly Csikszentmihaly, *Flow: The Psychology of Optimal Experience* (New York: Harper, 2008), 4.

Chapter 5

1. Marion Woodman, *Bone: Dying into Life* (New York: Penguin, 2001), 165.
2. As quoted in James Van Fleet's *Hidden Power: How to Unleash the Power of Your Subconscious Mind* (West Nyack, NY: Parker, 1987), 72. There is some question as to whether Einstein actually made this comment.
3. As quoted in Oschman, *Energy Medicine in Therapeutics and Human Performance,* 215.
4. Emily Dickinson, *The Complete Poems of Emily Dickinson* (Boston: Little, Brown, 1924), 330.
5. Carl Jung, "Psychology and Religion," in *The Complete Works, vol. 11, Psychology and Religion: West and East* (New Haven, CT: Yale University Press 1938), 131.
6. Linda Hartley, *Somatic Psychology: Body, Mind, and Meaning* (Philadelphia: Whurr, 2004), 101.
7. Bonnie Bainbridge Cohen, *Sensing, Feeling, and Action: The Experiential Anatomy of Body-Mind Centering* (Northampton, MA: Contact, 1993), 27.
8. Ivar Hagendoorn, "The Dancing Brain," *Cerebrum: The Dana Forum on Brain Science* 5, no. 2 (Spring 2003), http://www.ivarhagendoorn.com/files/articles/Hagendoorn-Cerebrum-03.pdf, Accessed April 4, 2017.
9. Christopher C. Berger and H. Henrik Ehrsson, "Mental Imagery Changes Multisensory Perception," *Current Biology* 23, Issue 14, (July 22, 2013), 1367–1372.
10. Ralph Metzner, *The Unfolding Self* (Novato, CA: Origin, 1998), 7.
11. As quoted in Rick Barrett, *Taijiquan: Through the Western Gate* (Berkeley, CA: Blue Snake, 2006), 181.
12. Joseph Chilton Pearce, *Biology of Transcendence: A Blueprint of the Human Spirit* (Rochester, VT: Park Street, 2004), 221.

Chapter 6

1. Susan Griffin, *Woman and Nature : The Roaring Inside Her* (New York: Perennial Library 1978), 226.
2. Carl Sagan, *Cosmos,* episode 9, 1980.
3. A. Bachrach. "Audience Entrainment during Live Contemporary Dance Performance: Physiological and Cognitive Measures," *Frontiers of Human Neuroscience,* September 2015, 179.
4. Carol Swann, "Key Principles," *Carolswann.net,* Carolswann.net/social-somatics/principles, accessed April 17, 2017.
5. Orme Johnson, "How Brain Coherence Radiates across a Population," *World Peace Group,* www.worldpeacegroup.org/radiating_brain_coherence.html, accessed May 1, 2017.
6. Tim Newman, "Gut Bacteria and the Brain: Are We Controlled by Microbes?" *Medical*

News Today, http://www.medicalnewstoday.com/articles/312734.php, September 7, 2016, accessed May 1, 2017.

7. Ken Wilbur, "What Is Integral?" *JoininIntegrallife.com*, http://joinintegrallife.com/what-is-integral, accessed March 1, 2017.

8. Mary Starks Whitehouse, "The Tao of the Body," in *Authentic Movement: Essays by Mary Starks Whitehouse, Janet Adler, and Joan Chodorow* (London: Jessica Kingsley Publishers, 1999), 53.

9. Helene Cixous, *Coming to Writing and Other Essays* (Cambridge, MA: Harvard Press, 1991), 50.

10. Jean Houston, *The Hero and the Goddess* (New York: Ballantine, 1992), 62.

11. Ken Wilber, *The Integral Vision* (Boston: Shambhala, 2007).

12. Amanda Williamson, et al., eds. *Dance, Somatics, and Spiritualities* (Bristol, UK: Intellect, 2014), xxvii.

13. Linda Hartley, *Wisdom of the Moving Body: An Introduction to Body-Mind Centering* (Berkeley, CA: North Atlantic, 1995), 303.

14. Brian Swimme, *The Hidden Heart of the Cosmos* (New York: Orbis, 1996), 112.

15. David Chalmers, "How Do You Explain Consciousness?" Tedwww, March 2014, https://www.ted.com/talks/david_chalmers_how_do_you_explain_consciousness, accessed June 16, 2017.

Bibliography

Achterberg, Jeanne. *Imagery in Healing.* Boston: Shambhala, 1985.

Auster, Paul. "Jonathan Lethem Talks with Paul Auster." *Believer,* www.believermag.com/issues/200502/?read=interview_auster. Accessed December 15, 2016.

Bachrach, A. "Audience Entrainment during Live Contemporary Dance Performance: Physiological and Cognitive Measures." *Frontiers of Human Neuroscience,* September 2015.

Barbour, Karen. *Dancing Across the Page: Narrative and Embodied Ways of Knowing.* Bristol, UK: Intellect, 2011.

Barrett, Rick. *Taijiquan: Through the Western Gate.* Berkeley, CA: Blue Snake, 2006.

Berger, Christopher C., and H. Henrik Ehrsson. "Mental Imagery Changes Multisensory Perception." *Current Biology* 23, Issue 14 (July 22, 2013): 1367–1372.

Blake, William. *The Marriage of Heaven and Hell.* CreateSpace, 2014.

Brande, Dorothea. *Becoming a Writer.* New York: J.P. Tarcher, 1981.

Brown, S., and L. Parsons. "Learning, Arts, and the Brain." *Neuroeducation,* 2008, www.giarts.org/sites/default/files/Neuroeducation_Learning-Arts-and-the-Brain.pdf. Accessed April 27, 2016.

Chalmers David. "How Do You Explain Consciousness?" Tedwww, March 2014, https://www.ted.com/talks/david_chalmers_how_do_you_explain_consciousness.

Chevalier, Gaetan, and James Oschman. "Understanding Earthing (Grounding)." *Earthing Institute,* April 2015, http://www.earthinginstitute.net/?p=2673. Accessed November 17, 2016.

Childre, Don, and Howard Martin. *The HeartMath Solution: The Institute of HeartMath's Revolutionary Program for Engaging the Power of the Heart's Intelligence.* New York: HarperCollins, 1999.

Cixous, Helene. *Coming to Writing and Other Essays.* Cambridge, MA: Harvard University Press, 1991.

Cohen, Bonnie Bainbridge. *Sensing, Feeling, and Action: The Experiential Anatomy of Body-Mind Centering.* Northampton, MA: Contact, 1993.

Collins, Sonya. "What is Your Gut Telling You?" *WebMD,* http://www.webmd.com/digestive-disorders/news/20140820/your-gut-bacteria#1, August 20, 2014. Accessed February 23, 2017.

Csikszentmihaly, Mihaly. *Flow: The Psychology of Optimal Experience,* New York: Harper, 2008.

Damasio, Antonio. *Self Comes to Mind: Constructing the Conscious Brain.* New York: Vintage, 2012.

Dickinson, Emily. *The Complete Poems of Emily Dickinson.* Boston: Little, Brown, 1924.

Eddy, Martha. *Mindful Movement: The Evolution of the Somatic Arts and Conscious Action.* Bristol, UK: Intellect, 2016.

Edwards, Scott. "Dancing and the Brain." *On the Brain,* http://neuro.hms.harvard.edu/harvard-mahoney-neuroscience-institute/brain-newsletter/and-brain-series/dancing-and-brain. Accessed January 28, 2017.

Elbow, Peter. *Writing without Teachers.* Oxford, UK: Oxford University Press, 1988.

Feldenkrais, Moshe. *Movement for Actors.* New York: Skyhorse, 2002.

Fraleigh, Sondra. *Moving Consciously: Somatic Transformations through Dance, Yoga, and Touch.* Chicago: University of Illinois Press, 2015.

Gardner, Howard. *Frames of Mind: The Theory of Multiple Intelligences*. New York: Basic, 2011.

Gershon, Michael. *The Second Brain: A Groundbreaking New Understanding of Nervous Disorders of the Stomach and Intestine*. New York: Harper Perennial, 1999.

Ghaly, M., and D. Teplitz. "The Biological Effects of Grounding the Human Body During Sleep as Measured by Cortisol Levels and Subjective Reporting of Sleep, Pain and Stress." *Complementary Medicine* (2004): 767–776.

Gladding, Rebecca, and Jeffrey Schwartz. *You Are Not Your Brain*. New York: Avery, 2012.

Goleman, Daniel. *Primal Leadership, with a New Preface by the Authors: Unleashing the Power of Emotional Intelligence*. Cambridge, MA: Harvard Business Review Press, 2013.

Graham, Martha. *Blood Memory: An Autobiography*. New York: Doubleday, 1991.

Greenstreet, Rosanna. "Q&A: Margaret Atwood." *Guardian*, October 28, 2001, www.theguardian.com/lifeandstyle/2011/oct/28/margaret-atwood-q-a. Accessed April 11, 2017.

Griffin, Susan. *Woman and Nature: The Roaring Inside Her*. New York: Perennial Library 1978.

Hagendoorn, Ivar. "The Dancing Brain." *Cerebrum: The Dana Forum on Brain Science* 5, no. 2 (Spring 2003).

Hanna, Thomas. "What Is Somatics?" In *Bone, Breath, & Gesture*, edited by Don Hanlon Johnson. Berkeley, CA: North Atlantic, 1995.

Hartley, Linda. *Somatic Psychology: Body, Mind, and Meaning*. Philadelphia: Whurr, 2004.

Hartley, Linda. *Wisdom of the Moving Body: An Introduction to Body-Mind Centering*. Berkeley, CA: North Atlantic, 1995

Hay, Deborah. *My Body, My Buddhist*. Hanover, NH: Wesleyan University Press, 2000.

Houston, Jean. *The Hero and the Goddess*. New York: Ballantine, 1992.

Iyer, Pico. "Writing Undoes Me." *Lion's Roar*, November 1, 2005, www.lionsroar.com/writing-undoes-me. Accessed April 7 2017.

Johnson, Orme. "How Brain Coherence Radiates Across a Population." *World Peace Group*, www.worldpeacegroup.org/radiating_brain_coherence.html, accessed May 1, 2017.

Joyce, James. "A Painful Case." In *Dubliners*, London: Penguin Classics, 1983.

Juhan, Deane. *Job's Body: A Handbook for Bodywork*. Barrytown, NY: Station Hill, 2003.

Jung, Carl. "Psychology and Religion." In *The Complete Works, vol. 11, Psychology and Religion: West and East*. New Haven, CT: Yale University Press, 1938.

Koch, Christof. "Is Consciousness Universal?" *Scientific American*, January 1, 2014, https://www.scientificamerican.com/article/is-consciousness-universal/. Accessed June 3, 2017.

Kornfield, Jack. *No Time Like the Present: Finding Freedom, Love, and Joy Right Where You Are*. New York: Atria, 2017.

Lipton, Bruce. *The Biology of Belief*. London: Hay House, 2008.

Lispector, Clarice. *Agua Viva*. New York: New Directions, 2012.

Lourde, Audre. *Sister Outsider: Essays and Speeches*. Berkeley, CA: Crossing, 1985.

Martino, Joe. "A Neuroscientist Explains What Happens to Your Brain When You Meditate." *Collective Evolution*, June 15, 2014, http://www.collective-evolution.com/2014/06/15/a-neuroscientist-explains-what-happens-to-your-brain-when-you-meditate. Accessed April 25, 2017.

McCraty, Rollin. "The Energetic Heart: Bioelectromagnetic Communication within and between People." In *Clinical Applications of Bioelectromagnetic Medicine*, New York: Marcel Dekker, 2004.

Mercie, Guy. *The Seven Mysteries of Life: An Exploration of Science and Philosophy*. New York: Mariner, 1999.

Metzner, Ralph. *The Unfolding Self*. Novato, CA: Origin, 1998.

Mindell, Arnold. *The Leader as Martial Artist*. San Francisco: Harper San Francisco, 1992.

Mindell, Arnold. *Working on Yourself Alone: Inner Dreambody Work*. New York: Penguin, 1990.

Murakami, Haruki. *1Q84*. New York: Vintage International, 2013.

Newman, Tim. "Gut Bacteria and the Brain: Are We Controlled by Microbes?" *Medical News Today*, September 7, 2016, http://www.medicalnewstoday.com/articles/312734.php. Accessed May 1, 2017.

Oschman, James. *Energy Medicine in Therapeutics and Human Performance*. Boston: Butterworth Heinemann, 2003.

Paz, Octavio. *Convergences: Essays on Art and Literature*. San Diego: Harcourt Brace Jovanovich, 1987.

Pearce, Joseph Chilton. *Biology of Transcendence: A Blueprint of the Human Spirit*. Rochester, VT: Park Street, 2004.

Pearson, Catherine. "The Benefits of Writing with Good Old Fashioned Pen and Paper." *Huffington Post*, September 12, 2014. Accessed April 13, 2017.

Pennebaker, James. *The Secret Life of Pronouns: What Our Words Say About Us*. London: Bloomsbury, 2013.

Pennebaker, James. *Writing to Heal: A Guided Journal for Recovering from Trauma & Emotional Upheaval*. Oakland, CA: New Harbinger, 2004.

Roche, J. *Multiplicity, Embodiment and the Contemporary Dancer: Moving Identities*. London: Palgrave Macmillan, 2015.

Rodriguez-Gil, Gloria. "The Powerful Sense of Smell." *reSources* 11, no. 2, http://www.sfsu.edu/~cadbs/Spring04.pdf. Accessed August 23, 2016.

Rumi. *The Essential Rumi*. New York: Harper, 1995.

Sagan, Carl. *Cosmos*, episode 9, 1980.

Schulte, Brigid. "Harvard Neuroscientist: Meditation Not Only Reduces Stress, Here's How It Changes Your Brain," May 26, 2015, https://www.washingtonpost.com/news/inspired-life/wp/2015/05/26/harvard-neuroscientist-meditation-not-only-reduces-stress-it-literally-changes-your-brain/?utm_term=.8d1d61335540. Accessed December 3, 2016.

Siegal, Daniel. *Mind: A Journey to the Heart of Being Human*. New York: Norton, 2017.

Snowber, Celeste. *Embodied Inquiry: Writing, Living and Being through the Body*. Rotterdam: Sense, 2016.

Sokal, K., and P. Sokal. "Earthing the Human Organism Influences Bioelectrical Processes." *The Journal of Alternative and Complementary Medicine* 18, no. 3 (2012).

Swann, Carol. "Key Principles." *Carolswann.net*, Carolswann.net/social-somatics/principles. Accessed April 17, 2017.

Swimme, Brian. *The Hidden Heart of the Cosmos*. New York: Orbis, 1996.

Van Fleet, James. *Hidden Power: How to Unleash the Power of Your Subconscious Mind*. West Nyack, NY: Parker, 1987.

Whitehouse, Mary Starks. "The Tao of the Body." In *Authentic Movement: Essays by Mary Starks Whitehouse, Janet Adler, and Joan Chodorow*, London: Jessica Kingsley, 1999.

Wilber, Ken. *The Collected Works of Ken Wilbur*. Boston: Shambhala, 2000.

Wilber, Ken. *The Integral Vision*. Boston: Shambhala, 2007.

Wilber, Ken. "What Is Integral?" *JoininIntegrallife.com*, http://joinintegrallife.com/what-is-integral. Accessed March 1, 2017.

Williamson, Amanda, et al., eds. *Dance, Somatics, and Spiritualities*. Bristol, UK: Intellect, 2014.

Woodman, Marion. *Bone: Dying into Life*. New York: Penguin, 2001.

Zohar, Danah, and Ian Marshall. *SQ: Connecting with Our Spiritual Intelligence*. New York: Bloomsbury, 2001.

Index

actions 77–78, 83
active imagination 128–130
Alexander Technique 3
articulation 8, 30, 106
Atwood, Margaret 96
Auster, Paul 98
Authentic Movement 3

Beginner's Mind 6
Berger, Christopher 126
bioelectricity 48–51, 57, 98, 127
biofield 50–51, 128, 139
Blake, William 51
Body-Mind Centering 3, 29, 152
body scan 69
bodymind 75, 95, 116, 122, 124; *see also* somatics
Brande, Dorothea 103
breath 53–55, 79–80

Cartesian thought 16
centering 57, 63, 75
Chalmers, David 153
Childre, Doc 49
Cixous, Helene 150
Cohen, Bonnie Bainbridge 29, 122
conscious embodiment 74–75
Contact Improvisation 3, 29, 131
Continuum 3
creativity 69–70, 71, 73, 99, 120, 121, 132, 151
Csikszentmihalyi, Mihaly 108

deep democracy 141
deep ecology 139
deep listening 3, 6–7, 10, 23, 45, 47, 52, 53, 67, 91, 104, 116, 122, 126, 145, 150, 152
delusion 117
Dickinson, Emily 118
doing versus being 65–67, 68, 70, 73, 130
dualism 115–116

earthing 56–57
Eddy, Martha 140
Ehrsson, Henrik 126
Einstein, Albert 115

Elbow, Peter 103
embodied presence 148–149
emotional intelligence 20
emotions 80–81
empathy 141–142
entelechy principle 150
enteric brain 49–51; gut 49–51, 147
epigenetics 73–74
evolving 147–148, 149

Feldenkrais, Moshe 56
Feldenkrais Method 29, 56
five senses 41–42, 52, 127
flow 75–77, 101, 108–109

Gardner, Howard 9–10, 43
Gershon, Michael 49, 51
Gladding, Rebecca 146
Goleman, Daniel 49
Graham, Martha 31, 63, 91
Griffin, Susan 138
grounding 55–57, 63, 75

Hagendoorn, Ivan 124
Hakomi Method 29
Hanna, Thomas 17, 19
Hartley, Linda 122, 152
Hay, Deborah 63
Healing Touch 3
HeartMath 49
Houston, Jean 150

imagination 113–115, 117–118, 123, 124–126, 127, 131
immanence 153
inner senses 47–52
intention 159–160
interdependence 73–74, 76, 138–140, 142–143
intersubjectivity 7, 62, 139, 144–145
intuition 19, 118, 122, 129
Iyer, Pico 88

Joyce, James 19
Juhan, Deane 49
Jung, Carl 120, 128

kinesphere 51
kinesthetic intelligence 10, 29, 43, 45, 74, 113, 122, 124, 127
Koch, Christof 153
Kornfield, Jack 72
kosmocentricism 153
Kurtz, Ron 29

Laban, Rudolph 50
Lazar, Sarah 39
life pulse 6, 26–27, 62, 64–65, 74, 75, 92, 146, 151
Lipton, Bruce 73–74, 130
Lispector, Clarice 94
Lourde, Audre 93

Marshall, Ian 43
McCraty, Rollin 48
meditation 3, 28, 30, 38–39, 71, 119
metaphors 126, 127
Metzner, Ralph 126
Mindell, Arnold 45, 141
mindfulness 28, 31, 78, 119
mirror neurons 139
multiple intelligences theory 9–10, 43–44
Murakami, Haruki 50
Murchie, Guy 46

nervous system 49, 72, 81, 130, 143;
neurons 10, 39, 48, 49, 51, 62, 89, 97, 104, 125, 178
neuroplasticity 10, 30–31, 39, 67, 146
Norretranders, Tor 129

Oates, Joyce Carol 101
objectivity 16–17, 57
Ogden, Pat 29
open versus focused attention 67–68
Oschman, James 48, 50

pain 2, 18, 21
panpsychism 153–154
Patrizi, Francesco 154
Paz, Octavio 18
Pearce, Joseph Chilton 131
Pennebaker, James 104
Penrose, Roger 153
perception 15–16
physical inquiry 26, 74, 122, 130, 138
presence 27–28, 69, 71, 90, 148, 149
Process Oriented Psychology 45–46
proprioception 10, 29, 40, 45, 46, 47, 72, 78, 108, 124

radiant awareness 143–145, 146
reacting versus responding 8, 21, 41

Reiki 3
resonant writing 90–91, 95–96
rhythm 97–99
Rodriguez-Gil, Gloria 51
Rumi 71

Sagan, Carl 139
scoliosis 2, 25, 88
Semmelweiss, Ignaz 117
sensorimotor psychotherapy 29
sexism 152
shadow 120
Siegel, Daniel 80
skin 47–48
Smith, Nancy Stark 131
Snowber, Celeste 89
social somatics 140, 141, 142
somatic attuning 52–53, 55–56, 71
somatic awakening 23–26, 29
somatic illiteracy 18–19, 52–53, 62
somatic writing 94–95, 99–101, 103–104; *see also* Hanna, Thomas
somatics 11, 18, 20, 25, 90; definition 17
Sontag, Susan 101
speed 78–79, 96–97
spiritual bypass 30, 149
spiritual intelligence 43, 151, 152
stillness 70–72, 88
subjectivity 16–18
Swann, Carol 140
Swimme, Brian 153
symbols 126–127
synergy 3, 7, 30, 99, 132, 178

Tai-chi 3
thriving 22, 143–144, 146–147
Trager, Milton 29
Trager Mentastics 3, 29

unconscious 118–121, 123, 129–130

We-space 145; *see also* intersubjectivity
Welwood, John 30
What Is 66, 70, 71, 75, 90, 92, 116, 128, 149, 154
Whitehouse, Mary Starks 150
Wilber, Ken 149, 151
Williamson, Amanda 151
Woodman, Marion 115
writing *see* resonant writing; *see also* somatic writing
writing from the body versus writing about the body 11, 99, 101–102, 103

yoga 29–30, 38

Zohar, Danah 43

www.ingramcontent.com/pod-product-compliance
Ingram Content Group UK Ltd.
Pitfield, Milton Keynes, MK11 3LW, UK
UKHW042015140426
5217IPUK00015B/1178